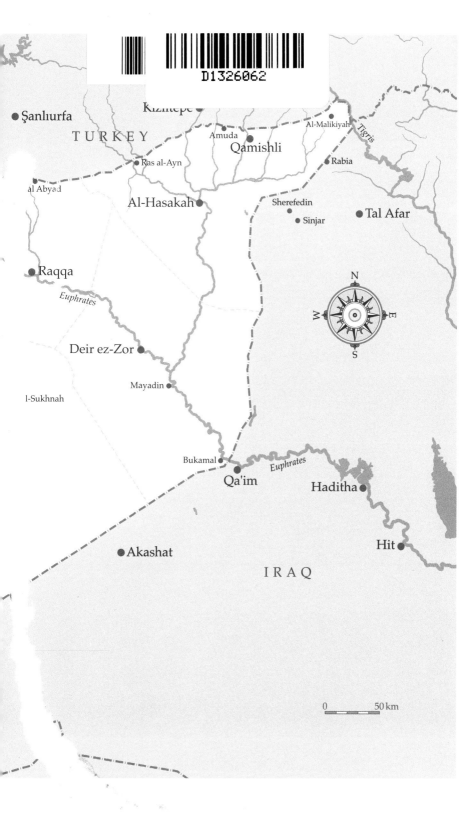

The
Book
Collectors
of Daraya

DELPHINE MINOUI

The
Book
Collectors
of Daraya

A band of Syrian rebels, their
underground library, and the stories
that carried them through a war

*Translated from the French
by Lara Vergnaud*

PICADOR

Originally published in French in 2018 by Éditions du Seuil, France,
as *Les passeurs de livres de Daraya*

First published in English 2020 by Farrar, Straus and Giroux, New York

First published in the UK in paperback 2020 by Picador

This edition published 2021 by Picador
an imprint of Pan Macmillan
The Smithson, 6 Briset Street, London EC1M 5NR
EU representative: Macmillan Publishers Ireland Limited,
Mallard Lodge, Lansdowne Village, Dublin 4
Associated companies throughout the world
www.panmacmillan.com

ISBN 978-1-5290-1231-6

1 3 5 7 9 8 6 4 2

A CIP catalogue record for this book is available from the British Library.

Designed by Gretchen Achilles
Printed and bound by CPI Group (UK) Ltd, Croydon, CR0 4YY

Visit **www.picador.com** to read more about all our books
and to buy them. You will also find features, author interviews and
news of any author events, and you can sign up for e-newsletters
so that you're always first to hear about our new releases.

There is no jail that can imprison the free word, nor is there a siege tight enough to prevent the spread of information.

—**MAZEN DARWISH**, Syrian human rights activist, in a speech given on April 23, 2016, following his release from jail in 2015

The
Book
Collectors
of Daraya

PROLOGUE

Istanbul, October 15, 2015

It's a remarkable image. A mysterious photo that somehow escaped the hell that is Syria without a trace of blood or bullets. Two men in profile, surrounded by walls of books. The first one leans over a text, open to the middle. The second scans a shelf. They're young, in their twenties, one sporting a hooded sweatshirt, the other with a baseball hat secured firmly on his head. Artificial light frames their faces in an enclosed, windowless room, emphasizing the unexpectedness of the scene. A fragile parenthesis in the midst of war.

The photo fascinates me. I came across it by chance on Facebook, on the page kept by Humans of Syria, a collective of photographers. I read the caption: the secret library of Daraya. I repeat it out loud: secret library of Da-ra-ya. The three syllables crash into one another.

Daraya, the rebel. Daraya, the besieged. Daraya, the starved. I've read—and written—a great deal about this suburb of Damascus, one of the cradles of 2011's peaceful uprising. Since 2012, it has been surrounded and blasted by Bashar al-Assad's forces. The idea that these young readers are hidden in an underground basement as bombs explode above their heads arouses my curiosity.

What's the story behind this picture? What's the hidden angle? The image haunts me, drawing me like a magnet to an inaccessible place: Syria has become too dangerous a destination. It takes me several calls on Skype and WhatsApp to track down the photographer, Ahmad Muaddamani. Ahmad is one of the cofounders of this secret haven. Through a spotty internet connection, their sole portal to the outside world, he tells me of his devastated city—houses in ruin, fire and dust, and amid the tumult, thousands of books saved from the rubble and reassembled in a refuge accessible to all of Daraya's residents. He spends hours explaining this project to save their cultural heritage, born from the ashes of a town that won't yield. He tells me about the incessant bombing. The empty stomachs. The soups made of leaves to stave off starvation. The voracious reading to nourish the mind. The library is their hidden fortress against the bombs. Books are their weapons of mass instruction.

His story is riveting. It rings out like an ode to peace that Syria's leader is hell-bent on muffling. An underground chorus that the jihadists of Daesh want to eradicate. A new voice that sprang from loudspeakers at the early demonstrations of the antiregime uprising, and was nearly muted by the ongoing conflict. This unheard account of their revolution whispers: write me down.

It is a perilous undertaking. How can you describe something you can't see, that you haven't lived? How do you avoid falling into the trap of misinformation, knowing Assad is not the only one spreading it? Aside from the books they are reading, what kinds of ideas do these young men entertain? Are they really jihadists, as the regime would have us believe? Or mere rebels who refuse to surrender? In Istanbul, I calculate the distance separating me from Daraya: 932 miles. I study the myriad ways to get there. But there's no point. Since my last trip to Damascus in 2010, when I was living in Beirut, I've been unable to get another press visa to access the Syrian capital. Even if I could get to Damascus, how would I reach the trapped suburb? This fall, even the United Nations was prevented from penetrating the barricades, failing in its attempts to send any humanitarian aid. Is there a tunnel, a back road, a secret path? On the other end of the line, Ahmad confirms that every usual route is blocked. All that's left is the breach through Moadamiya, a neighboring town, used only by the most daring. Such a crossing happens at night, at the mercy of snipers.

But should the story of Daraya be buried simply because we can't see past the wall erected by Assad? Should we settle for being passive witnesses to the incomparable barbarism unfolding live on our television sets?

If we look at this city only as it appears on a computer screen, we risk getting the story wrong. But looking away would condemn it to silence. Bashar al-Assad wanted to put Daraya in parentheses, to make it a footnote. I intend to make it the headline. To find other images, to fit them together with that first snapshot, the way you assemble the pieces of a puzzle.

A few days later, I call Ahmad to tell him my plan, anxious to hear his response.

At first, there's a long silence at the other end of the Skype connection.

I repeat my request: "I'd like to write a book about the library in Daraya."

A metallic clamor chokes the line. Another night full of this constant terror and danger—how ridiculous this project must seem to him. When the rain of bombs ends, his voice breaks through. *"Ahlan wa sahlan!"* Be my guest.

Hearing his enthusiasm, I smile at my screen. Ahmad will be my guide. I will be his willing scribe.

I make him a promise: one day, this book—their book—will join the other volumes in the library. It will be the living diary of Daraya.

At first Ahmad is a distant voice coming through my computer speakers. A fragile whisper from a hidden basement. When I first make contact with him on Skype, on October 15, 2015, he hasn't left Daraya in nearly three years. Located fewer than five miles from Damascus, his town is a sarcophagus, surrounded and starved by the regime. He is one of twelve thousand survivors. In the beginning, I struggle to understand what he is saying. He mumbles, timid but keyed up, his words broken by the omnipresent crackling of explosions. Between detonations, I try to focus on his face. He appears on my computer screen, then disappears, at the mercy of an internet connection patched together from small satellite dishes smuggled from abroad in the early days of the revolution.

His image stretches and deforms like a Picasso portrait: round cheeks slant at an angle under black-rimmed glasses before breaking into a million cubic pieces and fading behind a thick black curtain. When the pixels come back together, I listen carefully and try to read his lips, chewing on my pencil.

He introduces himself. Ahmad, twenty-three years old, born in Daraya, one of eight children in his family. Before the revolution, he studied civil engineering at Damascus University. Before the revolution, he liked soccer, movies, and being around plants in his family's nursery. Before the revolution, he dreamed of becoming a journalist. His father quickly dissuaded him from the idea, having himself spent twelve months in prison for a simple remark whispered to a friend. "Insult to power," the court had ruled. That was 2003, when Ahmad was eleven. A somber memory that had burrowed deep inside him.

Then the revolution. When Syria rouses in March 2011, Ahmad is nineteen, a rebellious age. His father, still traumatized from jail, forbids him to go into the streets. Ahmad misses the first protest held in Daraya, but sneaks into the second one. He joins the crowd, chanting at the top of his lungs: "One, one, one, the Syrian people are one." In his chest, inside this budding revolutionary, something rips, like a sheet of paper. His first sensation of freedom.

Weeks, then months go by. The protests are unending, too. Bashar al-Assad's voice shouts menacingly from transistor radios. "We will win. We will not yield. We will eliminate the dissenters." Regime forces shoot into the crowd.

The first bullets whistle, but Ahmad and his friends chant even louder—"Freedom! Freedom!"—as other resisters take up weapons to protect themselves. Unable to imprison them all, Syria's president decides to put their town under lockdown. It's November 8, 2012. Like many others, Ahmad's family pack their suitcases and escape to a neighboring town. They beg him to follow. He refuses—this is his revolution, his generation's revolution. Ahmad gets hold of a video camera and finally realizes his childhood dream: he will expose the truth. He joins the media center run by the new local council. In the daytime, he roams the devastated streets of Daraya. He films houses ripped apart, hospitals overflowing with the injured, burials for the victims, traces of a war invisible and inaccessible to foreign media. At night, he uploads his videos to the internet. One year of paralyzing violence goes by, full of hope and uncertainty.

One day in late 2013, Ahmad's friends call him—they need some help. They found books that they want to rescue in the ruins of an obliterated house.

"Books?" he repeats in surprise.

The idea strikes him as ludicrous. It's the middle of a war. What's the point of saving books when you can't even save lives? He'd never been a big reader. For him, books smack of lies and propaganda. For him, books recall the portrait of Assad and his long giraffe neck that mocked him from his schoolbooks. After a moment of hesitation, he follows his friends through a gouged-out wall. An explosion has ripped off the house's front door. The disfigured building belongs to a school director who fled the city and left everything behind. Ahmad cautiously feels his way to the living room, illuminated by a single sliver of sunlight. The wood floor is carpeted with books, scattered amid the debris. With one slow movement, he kneels to the ground and picks one at random. His nails flick against the dust-blackened cover, as if against the strings of a musical instrument. The title is in English, something about self-awareness, a psychology book, no doubt. Ahmad turns to the first page, deciphers the few words he recognizes. It turns out the subject doesn't matter. He's trembling. His insides turn to jelly. An unsettling sensation that comes with opening the door to knowledge. With escaping, for a second, the routine of war. With saving a little piece, however tiny, of the town's archives. Slipping through these pages as if fleeing into the unknown.

Ahmad takes his time standing up, the book against his chest. His entire body is shaking.

"The same sensation of freedom I felt at my first protest," he whispers through the computer screen.

Ahmad cuts off, his face once again a patchwork of pixels. A detonation has interrupted the internet connection. I stare at the screen. I think I hear a sigh. He takes a big breath and continues his story, giving an inventory of the other books found in the rubble that day: Arabic and international literature, philosophy, theology, science. A sea of information in arm's reach.

"But we had to hurry," he continues. "Planes were rumbling outside. We moved fast, dug up the books, and filled the bed of a pickup to the brim."

In subsequent days, the collection effort continues in the ruins of abandoned houses, destroyed offices, and disintegrating mosques. Ahmad quickly develops a taste for it. With each new hunt for books, he savors the immense pleasure of unearthing abandoned pages, bringing back to the world life buried in wreckage. They excavate with their bare hands, sometimes with shovels. In all, they are forty or so volunteers—activists, students, rebels—always at the ready, waiting for the planes to go silent so they can dig in the rubble. They salvage six thousand books in one week. One month later, the collection reaches fifteen thousand. The books are short, long, dented, dogeared, damaged; some are rare and highly sought-after. They have to find someplace to store them. Protect them. Preserve this small crumb of Syria's heritage before it all goes up in smoke. By general agreement, a plan for a public library takes shape. Daraya never had one under Assad. So this will be the first. "The symbol of a city that won't bow down—a place where we're constructing something even as everything else collapses around us," adds Ahmad. He stops, pensive, before uttering a sentence I will never forget: "Our revolution was meant to build, not destroy."

Fearing reprisals from the regime, the organizers decide this library would be kept in the greatest of secrecy. It would have neither name nor sign. It would be an underground space, protected from radar and shells, where avid and novice readers alike could gather. Reading as refuge. A page opening to the world when every door is locked. After scouring the city, Ahmad and his friends uncover the basement of an abandoned building at the border of the front line, not far from the snipers, but largely spared rocket fire. Its inhabitants are gone. The volunteers hurriedly construct wooden shelves. They find paint to freshen the dusty walls. They reassemble two or three couches. Outside, they pile a few sandbags in front of the windows, and they bring a generator to provide electricity. For days, the book collectors busily dust, glue, sort, index, and organize all these volumes. Now arranged by theme and in alphabetical order on overstuffed shelves, the books find a new, harmonious order.

One last detail remains to be sorted out before the library's unveiling: making sure that every book is numbered and carries its owner's name, meticulously written by hand on the first page.

"We're not thieves, and certainly not looters. These books belong to the residents of Daraya. Some are dead. Others have left. Others have been arrested. We want all of them to be able to retrieve their belongings once the war is over," insists Ahmad.

I set down my pencil, impressed by his civic-mindedness and speechless at such respect for others. For all others. These young Syrians cohabit with death night and day. Most of them have already lost everything—their homes, their friends, their parents. Amid the bedlam, they cling to books as if to life. Hoping for a better tomorrow. For a better political system. Driven by their thirst for culture, they are quietly developing an idea of what democracy should be. An idea that's growing. That challenges both the regime's tyranny and the brutality of Daesh, whose fighters set the library of Mosul, in Iraq, on fire in the beginning of 2015. Ahmad and his friends are true soldiers for peace.

Another explosion rips through our conversation. Unflappable, Ahmad continues his story. He tells me how on the day of the library opening the celebration was muted—no fruit juice or streamers, just a few friends gathered for the occasion. But most important, yes, most important of all, that tingling sensation prickling in his chest again, like it did during his first protest chant.

The library very quickly becomes one of the cornerstones of this isolated town. Open from 9:00 a.m. to 5:00 p.m., except on Friday, the day of rest, it welcomes an average of twenty-five readers per day, mainly men. In Daraya, Ahmad explains, women and children are not very visible and rarely venture outside. In general, they make do with reading the books their fathers or husbands bring home, rather than risk the barrel bombs raining from the sky.

"Last month, around six hundred fell on the town," says Ahmad.

His friend Abu el-Ezz, codirector of the library, was a near casualty. In September 2015, he was on his way to the book cellar when one of the many barrel bombs being tossed from regime helicopters landed in front of him. These containers full of explosives and scrap metal fall randomly and are therefore particularly destructive. Abu el-Ezz was hit in the neck by pieces of shrapnel that affected his nervous system; he suffers from cramps that stab down to the small of his back. Ever since the explosion, he's been on bed rest in a makeshift clinic.

Detonations echo. The bombings have resumed. Ahmad continues. This time, he lets me know that he needs to end our call. We don't know it yet, but there will be many more conversations like this one. Much longer ones, in fact. In his shattered country, where virtual connections have replaced physical ones, it's common to spend entire evenings talking on the internet. But I'm anxious to visualize this extraordinary place. To discover the color of its walls. The faces of its readers. The titles of all the books gathered there, saved from chaos.

A video from Ahmad lands in my WhatsApp. Along with Skype and Facebook, this is the most popular mode of communication among Syrians. The short film lasts two minutes, with no commentary or subtitles. I soak up the new images flashing on my smartphone. Here are the young men of Daraya. Here they are in their sweatshirts and tennis shoes. Here they are weaving their way through rubble, piles of books in their arms.

Behind them, a scene of desolation. Gutted buildings. Sheet metal strewn about. Lacerated walls. Hills of concrete overtaken by weeds. And smiles on their faces, a small victory amid chaos, when they unearth new paper treasures. Here they are again, stacking books in the back of a van. Then, without transition, the image shifts to inside the library. The camera pans across brand-new shelves, lingering on the miles of bound-together words. In the middle of the room, readers are plunged in thick volumes, notebooks close by. As I review these images, Daraya momentarily becomes an open book.

Captivated by the footage, I don't notice the background music right away. I replay the video, to take note of every detail. This time a gentle and familiar melody grabs my attention. I listen carefully. I hesitate. A minute goes by. What is this mysterious tune tugging at my memory? Suddenly, I recognize it—the music composed by Yann Tiersen for *Amélie*, a French film released in my youth that many of us watched over and over again. Ahmad texts that he's a fan of the film's star, Audrey Tautou. He's seen this movie dozens of times. It's become his solace, in a way, in the persistent bleakness of these years in Daraya.

So far, yet so close. With a war between us.

Istanbul, October 20, 2015. On my computer, the Skype icon bounces amid a peal of ringtones. Ahmad's face appears. He has "good news" to tell me: Abu el-Ezz, the library codirector, is with him. He's doing better. After weeks of convalescence, this is the first time he's left his hospital bed. Our virtual meeting is taking place at the media center run by the local council, which speaks for the opposition to the regime. The center's not very far from the book-filled cellar. The internet connection here is more reliable, the generator less capricious. For security reasons, Abu el-Ezz doesn't want to video chat. I concentrate on his words, let them paint a picture for me.

"Books are our way to make up for lost time, to wipe out ignorance," he says softly.

Abu el-Ezz is twenty-three years old, just like Ahmad. Like Ahmad, his engineering studies were interrupted. Like Ahmad, he'd never been a bookworm. At college, he says, the required reading verged on caricature. Countless sheets of paper wasted to honor the memory of the former Syrian president Hafez al-Assad, who died in 2000. Countless sentences written to flatter the ego of his son Bashar. And so much white space, pages deliberately emptied of the memory of political prisoners, tortured dissidents, and challengers who disappeared without a trace. So many unwritten stories, mutilated dreams, and buried critiques—voices vanishing under the weight of a machine built to lie and to kill.

"Before the revolution," he continues, "we were fed lies. There was no room for debate. We were living in a coffin. Censorship was the glue of our daily lives. They hid reality from us. We were told that the Assads, father and son, were the representatives of God on earth. In the many official homages paid to them, we had to affirm loudly and clearly that we were willing to sacrifice our blood and soul for them. I remember one slogan we had to repeat at school: 'Assad forever.' He was the master of the country, of time, of thought."

Behind the screen, Abu el-Ezz talks with the strength of a survivor, revealing both his fragility and resilience. I can't even imagine the pain tormenting him. But he wants to talk about his new passion, books, not complain about his health. He dares to believe in the good they can do. Words can't heal physical wounds, he says, but they have the power to soothe mental ones. And indeed, the simple act of reading is a huge comfort to him, one he discovered as soon as the library opened. He likes to wander through pages. Skim without end. Lose himself among the periods and commas. Navigate unknown lands.

"Books don't set limits; they set us free. They don't mutilate; they restore."

I ask him what genre he enjoys most. He responds that he's a little interested in everything. His reading choices are eclectic, varying from analyses of political Islam to Arabic poetry to psychology. He references a book by the American author Tony Robbins, the title of which he's forgotten, which talks about personal fulfillment, the quest for self, and how to build your own solid identity. The opposite of what he experienced under Assad.

"Reading helps me think positively, chase away negative ideas. And that's what we need most right now."

And what about the other library regulars? What do they read? What subjects capture their interest? At first, explains Abu el-Ezz, everyone was getting their bearings, dipping their toes in. A book is like a precious relic that you're examining for the first time—it can overwhelm. The most curious ones pick a text at random without much hesitation. The shyest visitors, those unused to reading, are nervous, intimidated by the idea of even touching a book cover. But thanks to word of mouth, certain books start to gain popularity, sparking trends even in war.

"That's how most of our borrowers ended up reading *The Alchemist*," explains Abu el-Ezz.

"*The Alchemist* by Paulo Coelho?"

"Yeah, it's one of our most popular books. People pass it around. Some have read it a couple of times."

Maybe this international bestseller appeals to the library's patrons because it uses simple words to describe a notion familiar to them: self-discovery. A Spanish shepherd's journey from Andalusia to the Egyptian pyramids speaks to them. Daraya's young revolutionaries hear in this book an echo of their own perilous odyssey. They cling to it as if to a compass, perhaps because it contains a treasure particularly precious in their eyes: the idea of limitless freedom.

They read as therapy but also to make up for lost time. Among Abu el-Ezz's generation, which has only ever known the rigid dictatorship of the Ba'ath Party (in power since the early 1960s), the thirst for change is striking.

"Most of the readers are like me. They never liked books before the war. Today, the young people of Daraya have everything to learn. It's like all of us are starting over at zero. At the library, people ask me for books about 'democracy' all the time."

"Democracy," a word once taboo, is now perched on everybody's lips. Another book, placed prominently on the shelf, has proven particularly popular: *Kitab al Ibar* (The Book of Lessons), by Ibn Khaldun.

"Our readers have all skimmed this massive book at

one point or another. In it, a fourteenth-century Tunisian historian uses his own experiences to try to determine the causes for the rise and decline of the Arab dynasties."

In the midst of revolutionary uncertainty, this forerunner of modern sociology offers, if not solutions, at least ways to think about issues as fundamental as governance, power struggles, and economic development—essential fodder at a time when the shape of the future Syria is endlessly questioned.

As I listen to Abu el-Ezz, I realize the extent to which books are helping transport these young Syrians somewhere else. No partial views, no censorship, but rather a new world filled with words, stories, and reflections. The residents of Daraya are inspired by these narratives, reappropriating them at times. They are a source of intellectual sustenance too long withheld.

Before saying goodbye, I ask Abu el-Ezz if he thinks he'll go back to work at the library once he recovers from his injuries.

"Of course!" he responds, as if it were obvious.

For him, the library is not only a place of healing but also somewhere he can breathe—a hopeful page in the dark novel that is Syria.

D ozens of other readers take their turn on my screen. One by one, their colorful descriptions of beloved books unfold like pieces of parchment. They spend hours telling me about the love poems of Nizar Qabbani and the writings of Syrian theologian Ibn Qayyim. They share their new passion for the theater of Shakespeare and Molière. For the novels of Marcel Proust and the South African writer J. M. Coetzee. For children's nursery rhymes. They talk tenderly about Saint-Exupéry's *The Little Prince.* Praise the medical textbooks that help them better treat the wounded. These are all books that survived the war, which they picked at random from the shelves of the new library, windows ajar within the confines of Daraya. From afar, I hear their voices disintegrate under bullet fire. Unshaken, they claim these writings as their new ramparts. They've memorized entire passages when, before the revolution, they would have been incapable of quoting a single line. The conflict causing bloodshed in Syria has paradoxically brought them closer to books.

Reading is the new foundation for the bubble of freedom they've constructed. They read to explore a concealed past, to learn, to evade insanity. Books are their best way to escape the war, if only temporarily. A melody of words against the dirge of bombs. Reading—a humble human gesture that binds them to the mad hope of a return to peace.

In the shadow of war, language is all that remains. It trembles with every word—words of wisdom, hope, science, and philosophy—that resists the gunpowder. Perfectly arranged and classified on the shelves, these words are strong. They stand tall, imbued with truth. They offer food for thought, a sea of ideas. The entire world in arm's reach.

This fascinating resistance through books reminds me of an Iranian hairdresser I met fifteen years ago in Tehran's working-class southern district. She had transformed her beauty salon into a reading space for women. It reminds me of the book-bicyclist I encountered one day in the traffic jams of Cairo, who aspired to raise education levels by distributing free books. In Daraya, reading also offers a way to learn, to uncover history, defying time and ignorance.

This paper warfare is especially dear to me because it echoes a personal addiction. A book enthusiast, I remember trembling during my first visit to the Library of Alexandria, which had endured fire and destruction on countless occasions. I have dreamed of a trip to Morocco ever since reading that the library in Fez, the oldest in the world, had been renovated. Libraries have something simultaneously subversive and calming about them. I've always loved to roam between rows of shelving, breathing in the smell of old paper, listening for the call of pages.

In Istanbul, a city blessed with quite a few grand libraries, story time in the library section of the French Institute is sacred. My daughter, Samarra, and I never miss a session. At home, she's even made it into one of her favorite activities: every weekend, she lines up her dolls in her bedroom, selects a few stories, and plays French Institute. I like to cite a recent World Bank study, reporting that people who read books live longer and are happier. Do books hold, if not the key to happiness, at least the power to make us believe in it?

As the library in Daraya takes form in my mind, I continue to assemble emails, text messages, and photos to get a better idea of the town in which it's hidden. I sort through the images, scribble down dates, scan for the slightest detail, and decipher acronyms and logos, on the lookout for the tiniest geographical markers—anything to fill in the outlines.

On Google Maps, viewed from a distance, Daraya looks like any other Middle Eastern suburb: rows of grayish buildings lined up like LEGO blocks. Seen closer, they're nothing but skeletons, piles of rubble mixed with sheets of rusted metal and broken windowpanes.

Gradually, I'm able to sketch a map of the isolated enclave. Here at last is Daraya, an open-air prison less than five miles southwest of Damascus. To the west, Moadamiya, another rebel-held suburb, also surrounded by the regime. To the north, the Mezzeh military airport perched on a hill, which Assad's Fourth Armored Division aims to defend until the end.

I open a dictionary. In Syriac, an ancient dialect spoken by the Christians of Iraq, Syria, and Iran, *daraya* means "many houses." What an ironic twist of fate for a town with so few buildings left standing. Sometimes the bombings are so powerful they dig craters into the very pavement. The deserted streets in every photo are just as striking. Metal shutters closed, schools abandoned, bakeries at a standstill. Daraya is a phantom town, orphaned by most of its inhabitants. Out of 250,000 before the revolution, only 12,000—nearly 2,000 of whom are combatants—remain, explains Ahmad. Every time I get him on Skype or WhatsApp, I pepper him with questions. About the color of the sky. About the sound of war. About the smell of explosives. He's incredibly patient. His voice, barely discernible during our first exchanges, quickly becomes more confident. His words are less hesitant, his speech smoother. You can sense the strength filling him when he talks about his home.

Whenever the connection is lost from the force of yet another explosion, his voice comes in jerks and starts, blanketing my desk in Istanbul with small, unstitched words, defying the roar of helicopters, seizing rare lulls to slip in a coherent sentence. For hours at a time, he tells me about Daraya. Its diversity. Its two churches where the Christian minority practices its religion unimpeded. Its famous white grapes with long and sugary seeds. Its fields so fertile that the regime wants to reclaim them. But in this agricultural suburb, known for its sweet wine, even the flower buds are now an endangered species.

A term comes to my mind: "urbicide," resurrected by the architect Bogdan Bogdanovich during the Balkan wars. Yes, urbicide is quite right: the destruction of a city by any means. We watch in the West, powerless, as a war machine gathers steam. It demolishes dreams, devours landscapes, and crushes everything in its path to impose its own blueprint. This destruction is physical, geographic, and demographic. Erasure by force is a classic strategy of this world's tyrants, and Syria's president looks to have mastered it.

But why is the regime so focused on Daraya?

One night, in the course of one of our many conversations, I ask Ahmad this question.

Why, yes, why is the regime putting so much energy into turning this one city into a laboratory of terror?

Shaking his head, Ahmad takes his time before answering. "Because Daraya is not like other cities." Then he adds, "To understand its civic resistance, which stretches way back before the revolution, you have to dig around its past."

And Ahmad begins to tell me more about his town.

It was back in the 1990s. The country was slowly recovering from a 1982 massacre in the city of Hama, carried out by Hafez al-Assad's regime. The tragic event, intended to crush an attempted uprising by the Muslim Brotherhood, resulted in the deaths of between ten and thirty thousand people, though no exact count could ever be established. Despite the scale of these atrocities, they were quickly buried, left unsaid. Cell phones and the internet didn't exist yet, and the government had a stranglehold on information. The mere rumor of the killings was enough to reinforce the system of fear maintained by Assad's Alawite dynasty since it took power in 1970. In Daraya, the city of "many houses," 142 miles from Hama, the massacre was spoken about in hushed voices only once the doors were closed, the curtains drawn, and the children in bed. As elsewhere in Syria, the word "regime" (*nizam*) was uttered in whispers. Privately, Syrians would vaguely refer to "security" (*amn*) or perhaps the "state" (*dawlé*). But when the sun emerged, the night would swallow these words.

And then, in the late nineties, some thirty activists from Daraya broke the wall of fear. They held secret meetings in the same mosque, one of their rare refuges. The imam presiding there was a progressive cleric. Seated cross-legged around him, the activists would study the Quran and read banned works by religious dissidents. In particular, they spent hours dissecting the writings of Jawdat Said, a Syrian Mahatma Gandhi and one of the first Muslim thinkers to engage with the notion of nonviolence. Contrary to the "terrorist" label they would inherit much later, these men were advocating a form of Sunnism favoring dialogue and tolerance. Their only weapons were a few secretly gathered books.

One day, they decided to take action by launching a series of public initiatives inspired by their readings: awareness campaigns to protect the environment, neighborhood mobilization to clean the streets, a battle against corruption. Thanks to their studies, a new kind of civic movement began to stir.

Ahmad hadn't been born yet when the Hama massacre occurred. He is also too young to remember the Daraya activists. Nonetheless, when he talks about this legendary period, it's with the precision of a good student. "This siege paradoxically forced us to open the doors to our past. I've learned a lot since 2012," he confides.

He has one person to thank for these belated lessons in Daraya's contemporary history: Muhammad Shihadeh, a companion of the siege, thirty-seven years old. Ahmad and his young friends have nicknamed him "Ustez"— Professor—because he teaches them English in the basement library. The name is also a sign of respect for this older man who was one of the pillars of Daraya's famous resistance group, known as Daraya Shebab (Daraya Youth). Between barrel bombings, sometimes in the deep of night, Ustez opens up to his young students. He talks of the first faltering steps of Daraya's nonviolent resistance, its discreet insubordination toward the regime more than a decade before the Arab Spring spread to Syria. Ahmad never tires of listening to him. Ustez is, in a way, the mentor of whom he's always dreamed—a bearer of knowledge, the likes of which the Assad clan never tolerated, neither the father, Hafez, nor the son, Bashar, who, when he took power in 2000, quickly quashed emerging hopes for a more democratic government during a short-lived period dubbed the Damascus Spring. For hours on end, Ustez patiently describes disappointed hopes, aborted attempts at change, and the resilience of the dissenters. Thanks to his lessons, a new world looms on the horizon: a world of questioning, dialogue, and tolerance.

"We owe him a lot," says my young friend.

Ahmad wants badly to introduce him to me, but regular bombings make this impossible. For now, Ahmad focuses on passing along his mentor's ideas. As if reciting a forbidden poem, he proceeds, soberly and precisely, to recount Ustez's shared memories, for the sake of remembering.

April 2002 provided an opportunity to hold Daraya's first protest. Israeli forces had just invaded the Jenin refugee camp in the West Bank. Ustez and his associates gambled that they could mobilize the population. Fearful of retaliation, they held the demonstration in silence, with just a few signs carried aloft. Some denounced the Israeli invasion. Others called for general "change." In many cases, the slogans borrowed from Quranic verses that could be interpreted as "God can do nothing for you until you change yourself." Even more implicit was the idea that the problem wasn't Israel, or even Assad directly. As Ustez later explained to Ahmad: "Our problem was our cowardice, our lack of education, our lack of courage to get things moving." That day, more than two hundred people, including a dozen women, participated in the procession. The police kept their distance. Without batting an eye. Forty minutes of freedom stolen from the dictatorship. A tiny victory over fear.

Ahmad talks and I keep quiet. He lays out the stories of those years with a blend of envy and admiration. The exactness of his account is the mark of someone who wants to grow from the experiences of others.

One year later, in 2003, the U.S. intervention in Iraq reenergized the demonstrators. This time, they organized a civil campaign to boycott cigarettes manufactured in the United States. On April 9, once again, people took to the streets for a silent march against the occupation of a neighboring country. For once, their mobilization echoed the regime's stance. Damascus was also opposed to the American operation. The mufti of Syria, reputedly close to the authorities, even declared a fatwa in favor of jihad in Iraq. The dissenters of Daraya therefore felt comfortable, safe even, in demonstrating.

But the government began to worry about this popular momentum, which, in its eyes, was growing too large. One month later, twenty-four activists involved in planning the demonstration were arrested and then imprisoned for "attempts to overthrow the system." They included Muhammad Shihadeh, who paid a stiff price: three months of brutal interrogations, before being sentenced to three years of incarceration in the infamous Sednaya Prison. The ordeal was painful but highly edifying. Behind bars, Ustez encountered members of the Muslim Brotherhood and Salafists, and also jihadists back from Iraq and Afghanistan. The same jihadists whom Assad later deliberately liberated from prison during the 2011 revolution, at the same time that pacifist demonstrators were being arrested. In confinement at Sednaya, Ustez met major opposition figures, like the communist leader Abdul Aziz al-Khair. And inside Sednaya, he learned to take refuge in books—an experience that would later inspire his young friends, even if he didn't directly participate in the creation of the Daraya library.

In 2005, Muhammad Shihadeh was released six months earlier than expected. The former prime minister of Lebanon Rafic Hariri had just been assassinated in Beirut. Blamed for the act, the Syrian regime found itself under international pressure. Assad pardoned a few prisoners to improve his image. The pressure nonetheless stayed on. Every two months, Ustez was summoned by the intelligence services. He was forbidden to leave the country. The university wanted nothing more to do with him. But he was undaunted. Carrying a diploma in English literature, he became a translator. He fell in love, married, and started a family. "More than a model," says Ahmad, "a source of inspiration."

In Daraya, several years went by in relative calm. Then, in March 2011, at the beginning of the Arab Spring, a new event rattled its inhabitants. In Daraa, another Syrian city, some teenagers had scrawled "Your turn will come, Doctor" on their school's wall. The message was aimed directly at Bashar al-Assad, inspired by the fall of Ben Ali in Tunisia and Hosni Mubarak in Egypt. The bold youths were arrested and tortured, plunging their parents into profound distress. Anger quickly poured into the streets throughout Syria. Fed by the contagious fervor spreading through the Arab-Muslim world, other cities joined the movement. True to its trailblazing past, Daraya was one of the first to rise. On Friday, March 25, Daraya Shebab, the movement formed in the nineties, regrouped for a new struggle. Ustez hurriedly wrote one of the first slogans. "From Daraya to Daraa, a dignified people," the protesters repeated in chorus. The crowd swelled visibly. In the space of one hour, thousands braved the ban on demonstrating. A success.

The young generation quickly followed suit. Against his father's will, Ahmad joined the second protest. He remembers everything about his "first time." His heart afire. Losing his voice from too much shouting. And quite simply the joy of being there. Myriad images flood his memory. Women throwing rice at the crowd, like at a wedding. Children astride shoulders, eyes turned to the future. Members of the Druze and Christian minorities, there to support a revolution that the Alawite Assad immediately labeled "Sunni" to divide Syrians. And the cri de coeur chanted in unison: "*Jenna! Jenna!*" Paradise! Paradise! The resistance of the nineties had passed the baton.

"People were yelling with all their might. An incredible feeling. We were one against the dictatorship. At first, we weren't demanding the end of the regime; we wanted more justice, equality, answers to our needs. And then everything suddenly shifted toward an unknown future."

When the first bullets whistled, the young protesters got creative: they offered the soldiers roses and bottles of water with a short note around the neck—"We are your brothers. Don't kill us. The nation is large enough for all of us." The idea came from Ghiyath Mattar, a twenty-six-year-old tailor. His message irritated the regime. It contradicted the official propaganda that saw hate-filled religious fanatics, armed to the teeth, scattered in these hordes of dissenters. On September 6, 2011, Ghiyath Mattar was arrested. Three days later, his tortured body was returned to his family. The young man had been castrated, his throat slashed. The death by torture of "Little Gandhi," as he was nicknamed by Ahmad and his friends, was merely a sample of the regime's unspeakable brutality.

Behind closed doors, some inhabitants started to arm themselves, discreetly. There were whispers of defection within the military establishment, and even insurrection. Ahmad and the majority of Daraya's revolutionaries refused to fall into the trap of violence. At every new gathering, the marching order was unerring: "*Silmiya, Silmiya* [peaceful, peaceful], even if they kill us by the hundreds." Faithful to the civic spirit of Ustez and the older rebels, they held the course of their peaceful mobilization: Ahmad's tireless group took turns protecting public buildings, participated in discussion forums, and even started an underground journal called *Enab Baladi* (The Grapes of My Land) to provide residents with important facts about their wartime situation. They became experts in "flying protests," when a group of demonstrators swiftly forms and dissipates just as quickly. They began to march at night when the daytime became too dangerous. Funeral services for "martyrs" even provided new opportunities to assemble. But the regime has as little respect for the dead as it does for the living. In February 2012, tanks from the neighboring Mezzeh air force base turned up in the middle of a funeral. Some thirty people were killed. "The incident is etched in our memories. We still call it 'Black Saturday,'" says Ahmad.

And then, the unthinkable happened. On August 25, 2012, the tanks returned to town. "It was in the middle of Ramadan," remembers Ahmad. After three days of intense bombing, regime soldiers attacked Daraya. Street by street. House by house. The inhabitants who resisted were lined up in front of a wall and shot, one by one. Men, women, children, indiscriminately. A collective punishment for the demonstrators. For the flowers and bottles of water. For the grains of rice at processions. For this peace odyssey that stretches back to the nineties, far before the revolution. Shut up in a makeshift shelter, Ahmad didn't discover the scale of the massacre until the troops left three days later. The bodies of dozens of victims had been gathered in the courtyard of a mosque. A cemetery was hastily created for some five hundred martyrs. "In reality, the dead probably numbered seven hundred, if you take into account all the others, buried when and where they were executed," clarifies Ahmad.

The death toll also doesn't include the countless activists arrested during the roundup whose tortured bodies turned up, three years later, in a file labeled "Caesar," the code name of a former military police photographer who took pictures of thousands of corpses.

"I was beside myself. I no longer recognized my town. My neighborhood," says Ahmad.

As he watched, distraught, columns of families began an exodus after the carnage. But the core of the resistance chose to stay and get organized. In October, a local council was created. By joint agreement, the two brigades newly created to defend the town, as part of the Free Syrian Army, the embryo of the armed opposition, were placed under the council's control. Another detail that set civic action in Daraya apart from that in other towns.

Bashar al-Assad doesn't like being resisted. On November 8, 2012, he retaliated again, this time imposing a blockade on Daraya. As soon as this sanction was announced, a new wave of departures began. It included Ahmad's parents. They begged him to follow them. Though he had no idea what lay ahead, the young activist made the choice to stay.

"You don't abandon a revolution halfway through," he insists.

He couldn't have imagined what would come next. A year later, as Daraya's remaining inhabitants were struggling to survive, two missiles pierced the sky in the middle of the night of August 21, 2013. Strangely, no detonations sounded. But in the span of a few minutes the community clinic found itself flooded with patients presenting the same symptoms: convulsions, pupillary contractions, feelings of suffocation. Like other rebel towns bordering Damascus, Daraya was the victim of a chemical weapon attack. In Daraya, as in Zamalka, Douma, and Moadamiya, the missiles had unleashed a horrifically noxious gas that would be quickly identified by French intelligence services as sarin.

Discussions among Paris, London, and Washington commenced. They decided to bypass the United Nations Security Council, subject to Russian and Chinese vetoes, and sanction the Syrian regime, even if it meant proceeding to strikes. Initially enthusiastic, U.S. president Barack Obama walked back his decision and left it up to Congress, after the British Parliament voted against action in Syria.

Ultimately, Obama yielded to opposition to a military intervention. Following a proposal made by Moscow, Syria's chemical arsenal was then placed under international monitoring, in anticipation of its destruction. A default retaliatory measure for which the inhabitants of Daraya paid a heavy price. After the infamous attack, the rebel town became the site of new atrocities. Unpunished for his crimes, Bashar al-Assad intensified his tactics of repression, tightening the noose around Ahmad and the remaining dissidents' throats.

"But we had to hold strong. Not let ourselves be beaten. Continue to carve the path laid out by Ustez," he continues.

And so one day in late 2013, the idea of saving books from the rubble emerged. Hesitant at first, Ahmad eventually let himself be convinced. What better way to defy Syria's leader than to contradict his narrative of a terrorist opposition? Bashar al-Assad had gambled that he could bury them all alive. Bury the town itself, and its remaining inhabitants. Its houses. Its trees. Its grapes. Its books.

From the ruins, a fortress of paper would arise.

The secret library of Daraya.

At the end of October 2015, I open my inbox to find a message from Ahmad, with the subject line "Library rules." I read:

1. No book can be borrowed without the librarians' permission.
2. Do not forget to return your books on the indicated date.
3. Any reader who returns a book overdue will be barred from borrowing others.
4. Respect the peace and quiet of others and abstain from making noise.
5. Be mindful of keeping the library clean.
6. Please return books to their original place after reading them.

In a postscript, Ahmad explains that these instructions were printed on an A4 piece of paper and prominently placed at the basement entrance, glued to a pole, so everyone can see them.

He and his friends have created something extraordinary in the midst of a war zone, their library a land without borders. A string of connected continents. A secret hideaway where books circulate with no need for a safe-conduct pass or bulletproof vest. In this protected place, they've managed to establish an atmosphere of collective intimacy, as well as a sense of ethics, discipline, and, oddly enough, normality. There is no doubt that this is what helps them hang on. Even the fighters of the Free Syrian Army are regulars at the library.

"Our most faithful reader is an armed rebel. He can't get enough. He reads everything he finds. He spends so much time plunged in books by the Tunisian historian Ibn Khaldun that my friends and I call him by that name now," jokes Ahmad.

The next day, Ahmad introduces me to Omar Abu Anas, aka Ibn Khaldun. Same setup as usual. A computer. Two chairs facing each other. The crackling of war as background music.

"*Ahlan wa sahlan*," says Omar.

He talks in a highly polished Syrian dialect, close to literary Arabic, as if reading great scholars has rubbed off on his vocabulary. Between two pixelated clouds, I make out his face, covered by a thin beard. I listen closely, relying on the precious aid of a translator friend of mine named Sarah.

Omar had also planned on an engineering career. Before the revolution. Before the conflict turned his life upside down.

"When the regime forces started to shoot at us, we had no choice but to protect the demonstrators. So I gave up my studies and volunteered to fight. It was the first time that I took up arms."

Twenty-four years old, Omar belongs to the Liwa Shuhada al-Islam rebels. Along with Ajnad al-Sham, it is one of two brigades of the Free Syrian Army's southern front. This young accidental fighter is one of the countless children of Daraya, aged eighteen to twenty-eight, who were propelled overnight to the front lines of the war. Unlike their leaders, deserters from the official army, they have no combat experience. Former college classmates and next-door neighbors, they sometimes find themselves fighting the bombs and tanks with one weapon shared among three people.

Liwa Shuhada al-Islam translates to "The Martyrs of Islam Brigade."

"Do you consider yourself a jihadist?"

I provoke him on purpose, as much out of curiosity as a desire for objectivity. And also from a need to clarify labels in the face of repeated accusations from Damascus. My question prompts a long silence. His face darkens. I imagine he's offended. Omar takes a deep breath before calmly explaining:

"If I chose to fight against the regime, it was to defend my land. My country. My right to freedom. Fighting wasn't a choice. It was a necessity. When your friends fall before your eyes for having brandished a piece of cardboard calling for change, what's left, except the desire to protect other protesters? Sadly, that's how it all started. And then, with the regime's bombs, the vicious spiral of violence began."

His statements are lucid, stripped of the usual provoc-
ative and ideological jargon we've heard all too often from
jihadists. At no moment does Omar reference the "gran-
deur of Allah," "revenge in the name of Islam," or the
"crusaders' plot," expressions used frequently by Islamist
fanatics in their speeches and interviews. In fact, his words
reflect the same candor as the revolutionary slogans of
2011—the thirst for freedom, and recourse to weapons as
the sole means to protect oneself. On the other side of the
screen, Omar continues:

"As for jihad . . . To those who seek to tarnish our image
by painting us as religious fanatics, my response is simple:
we are Muslims. That's how it is. It's our culture. But we refuse any usurpation of our religion. Whether it be by the al-
Nusra Front, the Syrian branch of al-Qaeda; or by Daesh . . .
Those people don't represent our ideas. They warp them!
Don't forget that the revolt began with calls for justice and
respect for human rights, not for Islam."

I'm curious to know at what exact moment books began to have a critical importance in his life. Was it when
the library opened? When he read a particular passage?

"It was when I understood that the war could go
on for years. When I realized that we could only count on
ourselves."

From that point onward, books would replace the university he no longer attended. He would have to educate

himself. Fill the void that could be taken over by fanatics imposing their backward ideas.

"Books had a crucial impact very quickly—they helped me not to lose myself."

And so Omar began to devour anything he could get his hands on.

"I love Ibn Khaldun. I've read lots of political and theological books. But I'm also interested in Western works about international law and the social sciences. It's only by studying other schools of thought that we can prepare ourselves to establish a new political system."

He's been leading a double life ever since, between war and literature. A Kalashnikov in one hand, a text always in reach of the other. He even created a mini library on the front line: a dozen works perfectly organized and protected behind the sandbags. The concept inspired other combatants. When the bombs quiet down, they exchange books and share reading recommendations.

"War is destructive. It transforms men, kills emotions and fears. When you're at war, you see the world differently. Reading is a diversion, it keeps us alive. Reading reminds us that we're human."

For Omar, reading is a survival instinct, a basic need. On every leave, he rushes to the library to borrow new texts. Books take hold of him and they don't let go. Alone in the night, his weapon his sole companion, he reads. He believes in the magic of the written word, a Band-Aid for the soul, a mysterious alchemy that allows him to escape into unmoving, suspended time. Like Hansel's pebbles, one book leads to another. We stumble; we advance; we stop; we begin again. We learn. Every book, he says, contains a story, a life, a secret.

"And among all these, do you have a favorite?"

"*Al-Qawaqa'a*," he answers immediately.

Al-Qawaqa'a! *The Shell*. I know this book. I read it before the revolution. It's chilling. Terrifying, in fact. The Syrian writer Mustafa Khalifa wrote it after twelve years of detention in Palmyra, the terrible "desert prison." This semiautobiographical account is full of atrocious descriptions inspired by his jailers' barbarism, torture, and the nightmare of his incarceration under the reign of Hafez al-Assad. I'm shocked that Omar had the courage to read this chronicle of horror. As if he didn't see enough of it in his daily life . . .

"Under Assad, the father and then the son, the book was banned. There was so much censorship that we had very little information about the extent of the regime's brutality. Most of us really became aware of it at the beginning of the revolution, when pro-Assad forces began to brutally crack down on us. Today, it's important to open people's eyes to our past, which, in moments of doubt and despair, can remind us why we are resisting."

Despite the cruelty laid out in *The Shell*, Omar developed a special connection to the book. It opened a door to his country's buried history. Reading versus the memory-erasers, the chieftains of single-minded thought. I would later learn that this once banned book is one of the most read in Daraya. It is all the more precious because it was found in the home of the dissident Yahya Shurbaji, a friend of Ustez and a member of the nineties group. In 2011, he was arrested at the same time as Ghiyath Mattar, the "Little Gandhi" of Daraya. His family has had no news of him since. But his name has stayed on everyone's lips. And in keeping with the tradition established at the library, that name figures prominently on the first page of the book.

Omar is also particularly attached to *The Shell* because it reminds him of his own situation. How to survive behind bars? How to endure forced confinement?

He insists on reading me an excerpt:

I unwind the past and I dream of the future. These waking dreams have become a habit. They bring me great pleasure—they're my drug. I build the dream little by little, I arrange every little detail, drawing them, correcting them. I immerse myself for hours, seated or lying down, I forget the reality in which I find myself: I transport myself to a reality where everything is beautiful and easy.

Omar looks up, still lost in his reading. He continues: "*The Shell* is a mirror in which I can project myself. A protective bubble I create to be able to endure the worst. A suit of armor to protect myself from danger."

His unwavering faith in books brings to mind all the letters and accounts left behind by the soldiers of World War I. Like Marcel Étévé, a graduate of France's prestigious École Normale Supérieure, who devoured eighty books in two years on the front line. Or Robert Dubarle, the captain of France's legendary mountain infantry, whose wife constantly sent him reading material for the trenches. Then there's the famous Société Franklin, which bankrolled the creation of 350 barrack libraries. Reading to escape. Reading to find oneself. Reading to feel alive.

Among the young people of Daraya, reading has even more meaning than that. Here, reading is an act of transgression. It's an affirmation of the freedom they've been deprived of for too long.

Despite their complete isolation, their reading choices are more varied than those of the trench soldiers of World War I, whose books were regularly scrutinized by military leadership concerned with controlling ideas and dissuading conscientious objectors. In Daraya, there is no screening of publications: the activists and Free Syrian Army fighters who saved thousands of works from the rubble maintain their commitment to putting all of them on the library shelves. And thanks to those satellite dishes smuggled into Syria at the very beginning of the revolution, they can even download new texts directly onto their cell phones.

"My friends send me lots of books on my smartphone, after getting them online. That's a huge help, especially when I don't have time to stop at the library to borrow new ones," Omar tells me.

His dream? To get hold of a digital copy of Machiavelli's *The Prince*. When I hang up, I promise myself I'll try to find him an Arabic translation. And I imagine him returning to a front line filled with dangers that even the grimmest of books is unlikely to depict.

Little by little, the missing pieces of the puzzle of Daraya come together on my computer screen, in Istanbul. After Ahmad, Abu el-Ezz, and Omar, dozens more activists and rebels participate in our virtual dialogue. In order to corroborate the information I've gathered, I schedule additional interviews. I fly to Lebanon to meet the regime's fleeing opponents. I travel to Gaziantep, in southern Turkey, to question exiled representatives of the Daraya local council. I talk about the enclave with journalists, diplomats, and humanitarian workers. Back in Turkey, I meet activists from the citizens' movement of the 1990s. They're unanimous about what makes Daraya so original: more than a symbol of resilience, the town is a unique model of governance where, despite the war, civilians, and not armed factions, have the final say.

Meanwhile, my conversations with Ahmad continue.

The jihadist question gnaws at me. In Damascus, the proregime TV station al-Dunya keeps repeating the same refrain: Daraya is a nest of terrorists. They need to be eliminated. Taken down for good. The regime propaganda blindly sticks to the same narrative. But I want to be sure. Does the suburb of Daraya harbor, yes or no, Islamist terrorists, even if they're a tiny minority?

Ahmad registers my questions. And he answers:

"I'm going to be honest with you. At the beginning of the uprising, most of the protesters in Daraya were waving the green-and-red flag of the Syrian revolution. Then a few individuals started to carry the famous black flag stamped in white letters with the Muslim profession of faith. At first we let them be. After all, we had already suffered enough under the grip of a regime that forced a single idea, a single banner, on us. Furthermore, the jihadists claimed this black banner was the Prophet's flag, not al-Qaeda's or any one specific movement's. They were using Islam as their shield, a way of saying no to a crippling regime. Later, at the end of 2012, when Daraya found itself encircled by pro-Assad forces, a half dozen Syrian combatants from the al-Nusra Front made an incursion into the town. At the time, it was still possible to enter through the breach in Moadamiya, the neighboring suburb. The anti-Assad combatants of the Free Syrian Army were just getting organized. The Islamic State hadn't been born yet. We didn't know much about the al-Nusra Front. So, yes, people let themselves be seduced.

Young people especially were easily influenced. Out of ignorance, no doubt. And despair, too. Sometimes, simply in the
spirit of being contrary."

The new al-Nusra partisans very quickly began to
clash with Ustez's old guard. They accused them of being
Western agents, of insulting Islam, of being *kafir* (unbe-
lievers). There were tensions, a few disputes. In 2014, the
local council finally made a decision to stop the situation
from degenerating: it signed a common charter with the
commanders of Daraya's two battalions, Liwa Shuhada al-
Islam and Ajnad al-Sham, which stipulated that no other
entity could be formed without unanimous agreement.

Once again, the voice of reason prevailed in Daraya.
Unlike Raqqa, another rebel-controlled town stormed
by the al-Nusra Front and then Daesh (the latter made
Raqqa the Syrian capital of its caliphate three years after
the revolution began), the enclave was able to stand up to
the jihadists. Unable to gain a foothold, the al-Nusra fighters eventually disappeared. Gone for good. But if Daraya
succeeded in driving out the jihadists, it was also thanks
to a unique and unbending setup: military decisions are
made by the local council, and not the Free Syrian Army,
as is the case in most of the other opposition-controlled
enclaves. Despite the instability of war, this entity oper-
ates like an independent minigovernment, with a dozen

departments (executive, military, legal, financial, etc.) aided by committees tasked with public relations, health, and public services.

"I'm going to tell you a secret," continues Ahmad. "I had my period of doubt, too. Even though I was against the use of weapons, at the very beginning I was curious about what the al-Nusra Front had to say. There was something intriguing about the group. Their discourse was well-practiced. I naively thought that they had come to support us, to defend our revolution. After all, we shared the same desire to change the regime. And then they quickly showed their true colors: suicide attacks in other parts of the country, the terror forced on territories they sought to control, the murder of Free Syrian Army fighters. Even though their terrorist operations don't go beyond Syria's borders, unlike the jihadists of Daesh, they're trying to place a black stamp on the country. Their ambition is territorial and ideological, under the cloak of Islam."

Another form of urbicide, a religious version. A perverse desire to transform cities and trap people into a single way of thinking.

"Another unique thing about our enclave is that the anti-Assad rebels are all guys from Daraya," continues Ahmad. "Young men, with no military background, who took up arms for the first time during the revolution to protect themselves from the regime's bullets. A third of them are former students, like Omar. What's really absurd is that Bashar al-Assad accuses us of having been infiltrated by foreign fighters, when his forces are relying on the support of Russian planes, and militants from Iran, Iraq, Afghanistan, and Pakistan, to smother what's left of the moderate opposition. Through his propaganda machine, Bashar al-Assad is trying to convince the West that he's the sole rampart against Daesh. In reality, the government's brutality is only radicalizing its opponents. Instead of pulling out the weeds, Assad is watering them. If the regime really wanted to eradicate terrorism, it would have started bombing Raqqa a long time ago, not Daraya."

Ahmad breaks off. He's talked enough about politics. He wants to get back to the original subject: the library.

"It's our best shield against deception and ignorance. Our way of banking on better days. We have to cultivate patience. You went through this in France. The revolution didn't happen overnight. The other day, I watched the movie inspired by that Victor Hugo novel *Les Misérables* with some friends. Man, it was depressing! But, at the same time, I told myself—it took years, but France succeeded in getting what it wanted. Social justice, democracy, human rights. That gives me hope again. The same hope I feel when I watch my favorite movie, *Amélie*."

I stanbul, November 13, 2015. I'm celebrating my birthday with a few friends, along the Bosporus. A brief moment of respite from the hellish news cycle. Last night, two suicide bombings struck Beirut. Last month, Ankara, the Turkish capital, was plunged into mourning after a pair of similar attacks. While Damascus wages war against the moderate opposition, the monster Daesh is bulldozing its own path, increasing attacks outside the borders of its self-proclaimed caliphate straddling Iraq and Syria. Despite the gloom descending on the region, Istanbul remains a cosmopolitan hub where friends from Turkey, Lebanon, Syria, Afghanistan, Iran, Egypt, France, or the United States can gather for the span of an evening. It's that rare multicultural destination where everyone finds his or her place to heal from the wounds of war and exile.

It's 11:30 p.m. At the end of the dinner, a Turkish friend approaches me and whispers, "Did you see what's happening in Paris?" I look at him. He's pale, holding his smartphone. He hands it to me. Red alerts flash across the screen. Explosion heard at the Stade de France. Gunfire on café terraces in the tenth and eleventh arrondissements. Shots at the Bataclan concert hall. I call my parents, my sister, my friends. Glued to the phone, I mechanically repeat, "Are you okay?" The roles have reversed. After eighteen years living in the Middle East, it's me asking *the* question.

The evening ends in worry, with telephone calls and shared dread. With all those little words you whisper to yourself, to reassure yourself, to pretend that you're fine, or that you'll be okay. Waking up the next day is like emerging from a nightmare.

Except the nightmare is real.

On TV, it's all they're talking about. At least 128 dead. More than four hundred injured. And the claim of responsibility, in black and white, by the Islamic State, which declares that it wanted to target the "capital of abominations and perversion." After *Charlie Hebdo* in January, Paris is once again struck in its very heart. Injured Paris. Wounded Paris. It suddenly sinks in that violence has reached my home city. Paris has always been my invincible refuge, where I go to recharge between tough assignments covering wars, revolutions, and political crises. Suddenly, the lines are blurred. War here.

There. Elsewhere. War at home. On the street corner. War without a front line.

My daughter wakes up. I have to put on a brave face. Let nothing show. Look, it's Saturday, and it's nearly 11:00 a.m., almost story time, our ritual that can't be missed. Samarra and I skip breakfast, throw on our coats, and go down the stairs. At the bottom of the steps, I take her small hand in mine. Then we cross Taksim Square, walk past the *simit* seller, pet a cat as we enter Istiklal Avenue, and wind through the dense crowd of pedestrians.

At the French Institute, the flag is at half-mast. The garden is practically empty. Only a handful of children have shown up at the library, accompanied by their brave, visibly tense parents. Julie's here, too, the storyteller loyal to her job, despite the mask of sadness whitening her face.

We take our seats. Julie stands up straight before her young audience. With a slow motion, she opens a bag filled with books, picks one at random, and begins to turn the pages. From the first words, her voice envelops the room like a comforting blanket. To the children, she has always seemed like a benevolent fairy. Suddenly her stories make sense to the grown-ups, too.

I look around me. There's something calming in the perfect arrangement of shelves, the coats hung at the entryway, the small benches lined up in front of the storyteller. For the first time, I pay attention to another detail: the library is in the basement. Every Saturday, we walk down a set of steps to reach it. A protective bubble. Like in Daraya.

Back home, I turn on my computer, torn between the desire to flee the bad news and the thirst to know more. Opening my emails, I immediately see a message from Ahmad:

We're so sorry for what just happened in France.

In Daraya, we are by your side against terrorism. If our own suffering was not so deep and if the bombings were less intense, we would have lit candles as a sign of solidarity, but sadly we can't do much.

I hope that you're okay and that, wherever you are, you're not in danger. Know that we are deeply saddened by what happened. We offer our condolences to you and to all the French people.

We know that if France is in mourning today, because of this terrorist act, it's because you support our fight for freedom.

We are truly thankful for the help of the French people.

Thank you from the bottom of our hearts.

I'm dumbfounded. Ahmad lives under a steady rain of bombs. He's lost countless friends, hasn't seen his family in three years. His daily life in Daraya is a spiraling crisis.

Yet he took the time to write this message, to share his compassion.

Would a terrorist ask forgiveness?

Would a terrorist grieve the dead?

Would a terrorist quote *Amélie* and Victor Hugo?

On December 7, 2015, I receive a new message from Ahmad.

This time, it's a shard of a sentence, piercing like a bullet fragment. It fits on a single line: "The library's been attacked."

I reread it immediately, scanning every word, every syllable, hoping to uncover some detail wedged between one letter and the next. In vain. I hurriedly grab my phone to call him. His number rings but no answer. I open Skype: Ahmad is listed as offline. Then I send him a text: "You okay?"

Met with silence, I resend my question a few hours later. And I add, "Are you there?"

Later that day, his response finally arrives.

There he is, at the end of this patchy line, in this inaccessible and bruised part of the world.

He's there and it was a close one. In the middle of the day, a barrel of explosives struck the building housing the library, ripping off two of its five stories, turning the entrance into a mountain of debris. In the basement, the shelves have spit out their books. They litter the ground like flotsam, disarranged by the explosion, bent, wrinkled, mixed with plaster and broken glass. In the fall, pages were torn out. Covers dented. Dust has taken care of the rest, burying tables and sofas under a grayish blanket. Now it's time to sort the books again, to remove the broken fragments of wood. "But you don't need to worry, everything's fine," continues Ahmad. "Nobody was hit, there are no dead or injured. A miracle! And actually, we're already back to work, cleaning everything, putting every book in its place, gluing pages. This is how it is. Life goes on. They just ruined the main door, the one that leads to the street. From now on, we'll enter the library from a hole dug into the left wall. It'll be more discreet, better protected. And yes, the library is going to reopen for its readers. And if it's not tomorrow, it will be the day after tomorrow, *inshallah*. In the meantime, we still have things to read thanks to the PDF files saved on our smartphones."

Ahmad tells me all this in a sporadic series of texts. Now and then, to save time, he answers me using audio clips recorded on WhatsApp. Since the beginning of the war, this has been the best way to communicate intermittently with Syrians on the inside. You send your questions. And they get back to you when they have time—or a connection.

A modern answering machine that escapes the regime's surveillance.

I ask him if he thinks the attack was deliberate, if Damascus knowingly targeted the library. He says nothing. That's how he responds when he's thinking. Saving his words, trying to be objective. Then he tells me that he doesn't really know. Elsewhere, in the rebel neighborhoods of East Aleppo, in northern Syria, the regime and its Russian allies purposefully target hospitals, doctors, and ambulances. It's blatant. Premeditated destruction. Even the United Nations has recognized it. But for barrel bomb attacks, like in Daraya, it's harder to prove. The strikes are random. They're not precise. They can miss their targets. Yet another reason they're so terrifying and so lethal.

"Deliberate or not, this attack confirms how much Bashar al-Assad hates Daraya. He just wants us dead. It's obvious," Ahmad continues.

His voice lowers slightly, then regains its original strength. "If he could burn us alive, he would!"

This time, I'm the one who retreats into silence. I can't help but think of *Fahrenheit 451*. About the mad firemen who set books alight in Ray Bradbury's 1953 novel. About the special brigade that roams the streets to punish offenders.

I remember a sentence uttered by the head fireman, Captain Beatty:

A book is a loaded gun in the house next door. Burn it. Take the shot from the weapon. Breach man's mind. Who knows who might be the target of the well-read man?

And I tell myself that one day I'll share this twentieth-century work of fiction with Ahmad. A prophetic novel he can add to his long reading list.

Over the following days, Daraya sinks a little deeper into darkness. Blockaded by the government. Pummeled by bombs dropped from helicopters. Condemned to live like an ostrich, head buried in the rubble, in an attempt to resist. As 2016 begins, winter pelts the town with the same persistence as the aerial strikes. "Daraya, the city the sun forgot," as they say ironically, and bitterly, in a video filmed by the local council during the siege and posted on YouTube. In December alone, more than 933 barrel bombs were dropped over Daraya. Easily designed and inexpensive, these are the Syrian army's preferred weapons of terror. Is this the reason for Ahmad's silence? Since the attack on the library, he's been less talkative. I imagine he's overwhelmed, especially now that more bad news has descended: in January 2016, after numerous aborted attempts, the regime succeeded in definitively cutting off Daraya from its neighbor Moadamiya, thereby depriving it of its last source of external food supplies. There is now no way to leave the enclave. The side roads are permanently blocked. The blockades are fortified. More families, in a panic, packed their bags and fled at the last minute through the fields, bringing the number of residents down from twelve thousand to approximately eighty-three hundred.

In early February 2016, a friend of Ahmad's takes over our internet chats, bringing me harrowing updates. Shadi is a round-faced twenty-six-year-old, with a timid voice that contradicts his lumberjack build. Unlike Ahmad, he's not passionate about reading. But he does offer a new page in Daraya's story: the war through images, which he has been collecting obsessively since the revolution began. Images that he circulates on social media, forcing the world to bear witness. Camera always flung over his shoulder, Shadi photographs everything, films everything. He weaves through his battered town all day long to better document its scars.

His daily life can be summed up with one video, which he shares with me in one of our first exchanges. Barely a minute long, filmed in 2014, it has yet to stop haunting me. I watch closely. In a graying sky, a helicopter circles at low altitude, its menacing blades whirling. Suddenly, the belly of the metal bird opens, unleashing a cylinder equipped with fins. The lethal device begins slowly in its trajectory before accelerating in descent, nose-diving toward a row of buildings. I recognize Shadi's panicked voice, nearly lost in the roar of the aircraft: *"Allahu akbar, Allahu akb—"* A first detonation, followed by a second, rips away the last syllable. The image jumps under the double impact of the explosion. The camera trembles, topples behind a balcony railing, but continues to shakily film two large clouds thickening in the distance. The barrel of explosives fell several feet away from Shadi as it let loose its devastating metallic cargo. Behind the viewfinder, the young man pulls himself together: *"Allahu akbar,* Daraya, January 12, 2014 . . . I filmed the barrel bomb! I saw it right in front of me." In the distance, a voice responds, panting, "I wouldn't have the guts to stand where you are."

Gutsy, but in shock.

"I was in a daze for the next few days, unable to leave my house. The bomb fell so close. I was stunned," explains Shadi.

This is only the debut of a systematic barrel bombing campaign, and Shadi will record most of it.

"Over time, the fear subsided. I started filming even more. I rubbed shoulders with death so often that I lost all emotion."

When Shadi talks, it's with the precision of a miniaturist painter. Obsessed with sounds, images, shapes, and patterns, he is now well acquainted with every kind of deadly bomb that crashes from the sky.

"We recorded nearly six thousand barrel drops in

three years. Sometimes, as many as eighty fall in a day. When the helicopters enter the sky, we watch them and try to anticipate the strike so we can take refuge in the closest shelter. It's a difficult exercise. The barrel fall only lasts thirty seconds, which doesn't leave you a lot of time to run for your life. At night it's even worse. You can't make out the devices in the dark. People who have basements have set up mattresses there. Everyone else is forced to pray before they go to sleep, hoping they'll still be alive the next day."

Since this January 2014 video, one of the most shared on YouTube at the time, Shadi has recorded hundreds of tragedies caused by these cylinders of evil. He's still haunted by one deadly strike in particular, at the end of that same year.

"A father had convinced his wife and their twelve-year-old son to move into a neighborhood less exposed to bombings. He had just dropped them off in the new apartment so he could go pick up the last boxes when a barrel bomb caught up with them. The wife and child died immediately, buried under the wreckage. The poor man was devastated."

Shadi, who reached the site right after the explosion, filmed everything that day. He filmed the building, caved in like a house of cards. He filmed the husband, his face ravaged by tears. He filmed the volunteers from the Civil

Defense as they carried two long pink plastic bags. The bodies of the two victims . . .

"This man wanted to protect his family from the bombings," says Shadi. "And the complete opposite happened. Our lives are worth so little."

Shadi, who's lost so many friends, knows this all too well. He tells me that death even follows him to funerals. One day, he lost friends to a barrel bombing during a memorial service.

"It was August 2015. For once, I wasn't filming. We were burying a dear friend, Ahmad Mattar. We were in the middle of reciting the Shahada prayer. Suddenly, there was a rumbling in the sky. The ground gave way beneath our feet. Two explosions. I could no longer hear anything. I had dust in my eyes and my head was ringing. When I could see again, after a few minutes, I saw the motionless bodies of two friends. They had been killed instantly. The barrels follow us everywhere. They can surprise us at any moment. They never let up," he choked out.

Like many young activists, Shadi learned how to film on the fly. He is a farmer's son who quit his studies after high school to work in the food-processing industry. A reserved child who never dared challenge his teachers. A young man whose eyes were "suddenly opened" in the beginning of 2011, in the promising early days of the Arab Spring. "Before, I would watch the world comfortably from behind my glasses, without much second thought," he says. The images of the Egyptian revolt transformed him. "When I saw Mubarak fall under pressure from demonstrators, I told myself, we can do it, too. I had always thought that the story of my country was already written, that nothing could change. Suddenly, we found ourselves in the streets demanding our right to write it ourselves, in our own words."

When the uprising turned into war, Shadi joined the local media center. He became one of many citizen journalists, indispensable intermediaries providing information inaccessible to foreign reporters. To better capture images, he traded in his smartphone camera for a real one. Then, in December 2014, when a friend contacted him from Damascus to offer financial aid, Shadi responded without hesitation, "All I need is a Canon 70D."

This crucial delivery was incredibly risky. Accessing the besieged suburb required crossing the regime's checkpoints, then passing through Moadamiya before rushing through the last access point into Daraya. This mile-long agricultural zone separating the two cities is in the crosshairs of the regime's soldiers, who can shoot at any moment from their mountain military base. As happens often in war zones, where women are as invisible as they are effective, a Syrian woman served as "smuggler." The camera hidden beneath her veil, she undertook the night passage on a deadly road where so many others had fallen. I can only imagine her thin silhouette weaving between the trees, furtively crossing swaths of grapevines and olive fields. Shadi has never seen her, but he owes her a great deal.

"My camera's become my greatest accomplice," he says. "It never leaves my side."

Since then, Shadi doesn't go anywhere without his precious device.

He uses it to record everything to the smallest detail. The explosions of missiles. Facades riddled with bullets. Twisted beams and girders. Stone wreckage. Thanks to the images Shadi sends me, I roam the streets like in a video game, darting into abandoned houses, jumping at the sound of an explosion. Except that all this is quite real. Behind my computer screen, the war is live.

The images are often jerky, filmed in a rush. Very short visual testimonials, hidden snapshots of this ephemeral life. When bombs rain down, the camera trembles, pivots, steadies. Zoom in, zoom out. Shadi isn't a professional reporter. He's a witness. An eye that stays wide open.

In the rare periods of respite, time stretches out. At the library, which has finally reopened, Daraya's militants film and interview each other, though their voices are sometimes inaudible in the videos. In one interview, someone is wearing a clip-on microphone, but it wasn't turned on. In another, a thick blast of air obscures the conversation. Regardless of the footage quality, what Shadi and his buddies care about is shouting the truth through images while the regime's cameras are trying to muffle it.

A spirit of fraternity also emanates from these candid shots. These young men resist together, mature together, and live together, split up into small adjoining apartments in the media center. Sometimes, in the middle of a sequence, unexpected poetry emerges. A fighter slumped in exhaustion, legs stretched out on an old sofa, face bathed in light, is submerged in a deep and gentle sleep. A soldier resting before the next storm.

As I gather more images, the library layout becomes even clearer. The white staircase leading to the basement. The scattering of shoes at the entrance. The central pole and its list of rules on a sheet of paper. To the right, the reading area. To the left, a space intended for debates and meetings—a new, separate area, which I discover while going through Shadi's footage. I recognize Omar in one video. The fatigues-wearing Ibn Khaldun has thrown on a T-shirt to give a political science lecture. Twenty or so young men are gathered around him, sitting on plastic chairs. Ears perked, they jot down notes as they listen to the aspiring professor.

"Most of the town's professors are in prison, dead, or in exile," explains Shadi. "We had to find a way to take over for them, to make sure people were still able to study. So our young people started taking turns sharing their knowledge with those who don't have time to read. Omar quickly became one of our most esteemed teachers. When he's able to get away from the front line, he meets with his students once or twice a week."

Shadi shows me another video: an English lesson given by . . . Ustez! I can finally put a face to the name of this cherished Daraya professor. Round face, thin beard, striped polo shirt. Not too different, in the end, from what I had pictured. A marker in his hand, he fills a whiteboard from left to right with short sentences in Latin letters. "This is a library," repeat the students, deciphering the first line. Then it's time for exercises. The students gather in small groups of three or four, tossing out "How are you?" and "What's your name?" The dialogues typically transform into strings of wild laughter, interspersed with comments in Arabic, the students' language quickly rushing back.

"To be honest," admits Shadi, "people are less interested in learning a language strictly speaking than, quite simply, the fact of being here. It's such an enormous pleasure to talk about something besides the war. To hold a pencil. To fill a notebook. A feeling of normalcy. The everyday life that we're starting to miss.

"Once in a while," he continues, "the space even turns into a dance floor. We push back the tables and chairs. We roll up the carpets. And we start to dance and sing."

I play a new sequence he sends me. In the right-hand

section of the library, a dense crowd squeezes in. Hand in hand, dozens of men and boys rock their heads, then their shoulders, from right to left, then left to right. Standing on a small, improvised stage, two singers launch into well-known tunes with a microphone. Like a single body, the crowd starts to hum a jubilant melody. *"Jenna! Jenna!"* Paradise! Paradise! I recognize this chant. It's the chant of their revolution, suddenly resurrected in this basement. *"Jenna! Jenna!"* they repeat in chorus. A throbbing call of hope. The solace of a shout for freedom emerging from the depths of the city.

There's something else striking about Shadi—his sense of imagination. For someone who doesn't read, who's never savored the company of books, he displays a surprising ability to project himself elsewhere.

"You know, lots of times I'll try to imagine the bombing of Daraya seen from Damascus. Actually, a few of my friends whose families moved to Sahnaya, a neighboring suburb, get panicked calls when their parents see the barrels drop," he tells me one day.

The explosion of violence darkening the plains of Daraya occurs only a few miles, as the crow flies, from downtown Damascus and the luxury hotel housing the envoys of the UN. And, again, a few miles from the hillside of the Mezzeh military base, headquarters of the air force intelligence services and their sinister prison, and where the shellfire originates.

For Shadi, there's no need to look up at the hill to know that he's in the sights of Assad's soldiers. Facing these robotic figures, guided at a distance by Bashar, he knows he's in constant danger. He is Shadi, the son of a farmer, an inspired cameraman, a militant for freedom. To them, he's just one more shadow, or worse, an "extremist" to be killed, a dangerous enemy within cannon reach. A bullet, missile, or bomb can bring him down in a fraction of a second. Shadi, a mortal among mortals . . .

"We've learned to live with the idea that death is at the street corner, that it could visit us at home, in our houses, as we sleep. Or in the mosques as we pray. Death won't leave us. If I told you we're not afraid, I'd be lying."

Perched on another hill, farther east, is the presidential palace. The inhabitants of Daraya can make it out with the naked eye.

"And Assad," I ask Shadi, "how do you imagine him? Have you already tried to put yourself in his shoes?"

"Assad . . . ," repeats Shadi. "The problem is that he's wearing blinders. He refuses to see us and accept us as we are. It's like we're living on two different planets."

How ironic that a president who studied ophthalmology now seems to suffer from selective vision. Not to mention that Assad is known for being a big amateur photographer. While his opponents film the government's many attempts to kill them, the Syrian leader feeds his Instagram account with selfies with fans, poses near the front lines, and struts around with his wife and children wearing a custom suit. Hunkered down in his palace, a bunker measuring several square miles, atop a hill in the Syrian capital, he spouts conspiracy theories and refuses the idea of a moderate opposition. The syndrome of nearsightedness. Or rather of distorted reality, like the analog photos developed in a darkroom—easily manipulated. They can be modified depending on the effects of light and shadow you want to add. This warped vision has colored his words as well: "It's me or chaos," he repeats over and over, deaf to the opposition's calls for peace.

Among Shadi and his friends, creativity has no limits. They find enormous pleasure in exploring a new vocabulary, inspired by the roots of their rich Arabic language. While Assad speaks of "chaos" using the classical Arabic term *fauda*, they retort with a synonym, the more informal *karkabeh*—which can be roughly translated as "snafu"—to describe their daily lives under the bombs. This word even became the title of a bimonthly magazine created in early 2015, with the means at hand. With a circulation of only five hundred copies, produced with a photocopier saved from the rubble, *Karkabeh* is primarily a survival guide. How to burn plastic to make heating oil? How to conserve rainwater for drinking? How to grow tomatoes on your balcony? Everything is explained, in black and white, sometimes illustrated with photos or sketches, and distributed on the front line and among the city's residents.

The magazine also includes short news articles about politics, sports, and cinema for those who don't have the time or patience to dive into a long literary or philosophical work. "A mental diversion to try to get our heads together," explains Shadi. He, Ahmad, and other friends in Daraya created this self-published magazine to maintain a social connection and prevent despair from leading to radicalization.

I skim a few pages that have been published online. The "chaos" they offer their readers is perfectly organized, arranged by theme. Poems by the exiled Iraqi dissident Ahmed Matar are joined by texts dedicated to Ibn Battuta, the fourteenth-century Moroccan explorer; Alfred Nobel, the creator of the eponymous prize; the different Syrian flags in the country's history; the martyrs of Daraya; and the refugees exiled to Turkey. Raw stories. Neutral words. No value judgments or partisan stripes. There is no place for the vocabulary of threats and fear, prized by the pro-regime media, in this "chaos." *Karkabeh* also has nothing to do with the propaganda newsletters produced by the Islamic State and circulated in several languages on social media. No bloody death scenes or dramatizations. The articles are simple, stripped of all forms of provocation—apart from self-deprecation.

The only real danger comes from laughing too hard, especially when doing the crossword puzzle. Under empty boxes, which readers are invited to fill using only a war vocabulary—siege, bombs, soldiers, martyrs—the budding journalists have appended an "editorial note": "The magazine is not responsible for any fainting spells or heart attacks caused by this wordplay." Amid the ruins of their town, they are sculpting a new language of the absurd. Molded by reality, their writing is both tragic and comical. Here, real life reigns. A town telling its story as it fights for survival, making fun of itself, and mocking its fears and daily worries to better control them.

Another page offers the weekly horoscope. The traditional zodiac signs have been replaced by more familiar symbols: rocket, kitchen, rock climber, fuel oil, etc. The pseudoastrological advice is of course adapted to the particular chaos of Daraya: "If your friends invite you over for tea, better eat before you go. Otherwise, you'll starve to death." "Today's commute is hopeless; all roads closed till further notice." "You keep digging tunnels to protect yourself. But fortune may smile upon you: you will eventually unearth a treasure."

A little lower down, I smile as I read a second "warning" from the editors: "This horoscope is entirely a product of our imagination. Any resemblance to reality is pure coincidence."

It's February 2016, and the more bombs fall, the more life takes form below the surface. An underground world, in both senses, that sprouts a few stone throws from the front line. Library, schools, local council, media center, shelters, tunnels, etc. Even the hospital has moved its facilities belowground. "Now, because of the aerial strikes, our town has switched from horizontal to vertical," explains Ahmad, who's finally popped back onto my screen. "Daraya," he continues, "is no longer a flat ribbon dotted with 'many houses.' It's divided into three levels: the sky and the helicopters that chased away the stars; the ground, disfigured by bombs; the clandestine basements nestled in the shadow of chaos." To protect themselves, residents without basements hastily fashion improvised burrows under their buildings' foundations. Digging holes has become the fate of those who oppose Assad. More like a life sentence of forced labor.

With Ahmad and Shadi, I plunge a little more each day into the underground labyrinth of parceled-out images of this ghost town. They reach me in scraps, through the Web, in an organized confusion to which I've become accustomed. Small visual fragments that have survived the siege. Incomprehensible pieces of life that we put together one by one to describe the tragedy, madness, and hope.

Every video is a new discovery. I have a strange feeling that I hold the secret access code to Daraya; despite Damascus's prohibition, I can explore its abysses. Thanks to yet another filmed sequence, I discover that the book cellar has transformed into a discussion forum that engages both the activists behind the scenes and the fighters on the front lines. On this day, the debate is about how to evaluate the revolution. Were the demonstrators ready? Should they have been better organized? Could they have avoided the violence, the hundreds of thousands of deaths, the displacements, and the exiles? Despite the cruelty of the war, none of the participants express regret for having demanded change, beginning in the spring of 2011. Throughout the debate, the terms "right," "freedom," and "wake-up call" echo repeatedly. A young man stands up. "The revolution," he says, "put us on the right path." Another continues, "tired" but "without regrets." "Democracy," he adds, "remains an objective. A goal that's still developing." A third participant is more self-critical. "I would have liked us to be better prepared for this uprising, on the intellectual and religious level. We needed more time, both those who took up arms and those who practiced nonviolent revolution. And I'm not only talking about Daraya. Because of the lack of preparation, we're under constant pressure, inside and out." He's referring to the regime's brutality as well as to the theater of war by proxy that his country has become: Iran versus Saudi Arabia, the United States versus Russia, not to mention all the other actors in this conflict, e.g., Qatar and Turkey.

I observe this young man. He's wearing a khaki jacket and a multipocketed pair of pants, the uniform of the Free Syrian Army fighters. Is it the company of books that gives this anti-Assad warrior the perspective needed to fairly evaluate his side? Or perhaps it's just the library atmosphere that fosters exchanges and discussions of nuance and color, when Damascus only wants to see in black and white. And Assad's soldiers? What are they thinking about over at the Mezzeh base? Can they think in color? For that matter, do they have the time—and the freedom—to read books other than those forced on them? Would they, in their turn, be capable of aspiring to change if they ever had the choice?

As I reconsider this sequence, alone in front of my computer, a phrase from one of Kafka's letters to Oskar Pollak comes to mind: "A book must be the axe for the frozen sea inside us."

Over the following days, the messages from Ahmad and the others suggest that the time spent reading in the library has decreased due to the constant clamor of the barrel bombs. On mornings when the sky rages without end, it remains closed to the public. Sometimes it's overrun by the neighborhood children, who've left their makeshift shelters, consisting for some families of a miserable little dungeon, to get some "fresh air." One of the kids, Amjad, has made the library his new anchor point. His friends have even nicknamed him "the Librarian."

When the library eventually reopens its doors, in the slightest of lulls, the debate resumes with greater intensity.

Then comes a new video. The speaker is wearing a red T-shirt. He asks the participants to form small groups to which he hands out pieces of cardboard, cut into puzzle pieces. "You have forty-five seconds to reassemble them." After the allotted time, a single team claims victory. The instructor smiles. "Of course. That was the only team to see the model before doing the puzzle." His conclusion: "When you don't have a clear plan in your head, your ideas become muddled. If you define your priorities, you have less chance of getting lost." The room is silent. He adds, "Don't blindly follow others. Explore new spots, new places." Ironic for a besieged town, stripped of its escape routes. He keeps going. "Thinking is what matters. Don't let anyone manipulate you for their own aims." At no moment are the names of Assad or Daesh pronounced. Everyone gathered understands the message: refuse single-minded and destructive thinking;

don't fall into the trap of believing doctored truths. Bent over their notebooks, the participants scribble as they nod their heads.

Suddenly the light goes out. Squeezed into a corner of the room, an overhead projector turns on, transforming a white wall into a cinema screen. In this multipurpose library, they watch movies, too! The short film of the day is called *Two & Two*, the story of a primary school teacher who forces his students to repeat the false sum $2 + 2 = 5$ or risk punishment. This fable about the fabrication of a lie through force is a reference to the "false formula" in George Orwell's indispensable *1984*. The film, made by Babak Anvari, an Iranian director in exile, was downloaded from the internet. It contains a message of hope. At the end of the math lesson, a schoolchild huddled in the back of the classroom defies the established order by scratching out the imposed number with a pencil and replacing it with a "4" in his notebook. Rapturous applause in the room. Amid this hubbub, I read the following sentence, written in Arabic, that takes over the white wall: "If everyone believes in the same idea, does that make it true?"

At the bottom of the black hole that has been made of Daraya, these young people's resources are inexhaustible. In a sanctuary surrounded by ruins, they build up their frames of reference, explore new ideas, and broaden their cultural knowledge a little more each day. A clandestine life, in which the silence imposed from above turns into a cry of fury and courage. I watch them. They have the same spirit as that schoolboy resisting until the end: defying the diktats, refusing to let themselves be distracted by the noise of cannons, transforming the somber reality of war into a challenge they must over-come to better move forward. For the span of a movie or book, they strive to write a new page in the history of their country.

The path is steep, and they know it. Far from the often sterile discussions of the opposition in exile, far from the luxury hotels in Geneva and the corruption scandals, they advance with baby steps, preferring to enrich themselves from a range of ideas rather than come to hasty conclu-sions on the color of the future flag, the role of Islam in society, or the place of the Kurds in the future Syria.

The famous "Turkish model," held up as an example in the beginning of the Arab Spring, is of interest to some of them. They want to believe in this blend of "Islam, de-mocracy, and growth." But they are not totally convinced. "Can the Turkish experience be adapted to other coun-tries?" asks a Daraya militant in yet another video. Omar, the Ibn Khaldun in chief, answers him quite clearly. "Yes, but provided that we learn lessons from [Turkish president] Recep Tayyip Erdogan's mistakes." Once again, a series of questions follows. What comes after protest? How can we carry out the transition? What regime should be put in place? Can political Islam be reconciled with democracy?

Their thirst to learn is endless. One February morning, Ahmad reveals to me the existence of another underground discussion space, opened at the end of 2015. Maintained in the utmost secrecy, it houses a second debate room in which videoconferences are organized via Skype, for the town's inhabitants to talk with outsiders. Seated in front of a screen, they have carte blanche to ask any question they want to the teachers and dissidents of all persuasions who stream in front of their eyes. An opportunity to lay the groundwork for a political project that's more open and tolerant than the one in which they grew up.

"In recent weeks, we've hosted the secular opposi-tionist Burhan Ghalioun, and the president of the Syrian National Council, George Sabra," explains Ahmad. "We've even given the floor to Huthaifa Azzam, the son of a Palestinian jihadist, who rejected the violence advocated by his father—a way to dissuade our young people from radicalism."

Because of security concerns, no images from these closed-door conferences have left Daraya. To avoid attract-ing the attention of the regime, and in particular its barrel-spitting helicopters, the organizers have even returned to the old tradition of word of mouth when announcing the dates of the debates.

"It's the kind of university we've always dreamed about. A place to learn, without preestablished lines we can't cross, far from censorship, open to all viewpoints," sighs Ahmad.

This clandestine university is a place of transgression. Transgression through learning. The young revolutionaries of Daraya can at last chalk a new score on the blackboard of their dreams, a score whose notes sing of a better future—the fragile melody of a city surviving in the darkness.

When every door has closed, the slightest opening offers relief. In the seemingly interminable month of February 2016, Ahmad tells me about the book breaking all the records in Daraya.

"Have you heard of *The 7 Habits*?" he asks me one day, through our virtual window.

"The what?" I answer in surprise.

"*The 7 Habits of Highly Effective People*, by the American Stephen Covey."

He repeats this as if it were obvious. His country is at war. His city on the verge of destruction. Daraya is prisoner to explosions, smoke, pandemonium. And now, in the heart of their daily chaos—*karkabeh*—Ahmad is talking about some self-help book, one of many popular in our Western society where the individual comes before the community. This international bestseller, of which I've only read a description, talks about identity-building as a necessary stage on the road to success. A "step-by-step" approach, it focuses on the development of personal efficiency by which

"Save Syria" graffiti, painted on a wall in Daraya by
Abu Malek al-Shami, a cofounder of the library.

(Photograph © Abu Malek al-Shami, 2016)

In just one month, the young activists we now know as the book collectors
saved around fifteen thousand books from the rubble of Daraya.

(Photograph © Mohammad al-Eman, 2013)

Ustez—"the Professor," from whom the young men in the library learned not only English but also tactics of nonviolent resistance—searches for books. (Photograph © Mohammad al-Eman, 2013)

This photo, posted by Humans of Syria on Facebook, was the journalist Delphine Minoui's first encounter with the book collectors of Daraya. She tracked down their contact information and reached them a few days later via WhatsApp; they were in constant touch over the course of the rest of the siege.

(Photograph © Ahmad Muaddamani, 2015)

Activists and anti-Assad fighters were regular visitors to the library. "Books help us stay human," they used to say. (Photograph © Ahmad Muaddamani, 2015)

An English class held in the library, which, over time, became a kind of underground university. Every week, dozens of activists and residents came in for lectures on a wide range of subjects. They even managed Skype conferences with Syrian academics and dissidents in exile.

(Photograph © Ahmad Muaddamani, 2014)

The artist and activist Abu Malek transforms the ruins of Daraya with his work and gives hope human form with his graffiti.
(Photograph © Ahmad Muaddamani, 2015)

Omar, pictured here, a booklover and anti-Assad fighter, built himself a mini library at the front, with selected volumes carefully stored behind sandbags. (Photograph © Malik Alrifaii, 2015)

When bombs stop falling during a brief truce, the women
of Daraya seize the opportunity to protest against the siege, hoping
to gain attention from the international community.

(Photograph © Fadi Dabbas, 2015)

On the first page of each collected book, the young
librarians wrote the name of its owner in the hope of
reuniting them when the war was over.

(Photograph © Ahmad Muaddamani, 2014)

A view of the cloud created by a barrel bomb, which suggests the damage this artillery caused to the city. (Photograph © Fadi Dabbas, 2013)

Shadi's favorite camera helped document the siege. After it was destroyed during a regime attack, he was left with just his cell phone and mini Sony cameras.

(Photograph © Shadi Matar, 2016)

More graffiti by Abu Malek al-Shami. This one, painted in a destroyed school, reads: "We used to joke around and say, I hope the school falls down. And now it has fallen." (Photograph © Ahmad Muaddamani, 2015)

Every day Ahmad and his activist friends would survey the bombed streets of besieged Daraya to film and document the war in the absence of professional reporters and foreign media. (Photograph © Ahmad Muaddamani, 2015)

A group selfie, taken in the basement of one of the many houses that the book collectors searched. Among other young activists from Daraya, Ahmad Muaddamani stands on the far left and Shadi Matar appears on the bottom right. (Photograph © Mohammad al-Eman, 2015)

Ahmad's love of books is irrepressible. Within a year of the evacuation from Daraya, he and his friends founded a mobile library in Idlib, which immediately achieved great popularity among the children and women of the province. (Photograph © Mohammad al-Eman, 2016)

The author with four of Daraya's activists, when they reunited in Istanbul in 2018. From left: Ustez, Shadi, Hussam (Jihad), Delphine, Ahmad

(Photograph © Marie Tihon, 2018)

the individual gains autonomy from the group and learns to better manage his or her relationship with others. The book has been translated into thirty-eight languages, including Arabic. But still, what a surprise to find a book common in the business milieus of Paris, London, New York, and Dubai in a Syrian battle zone.

"This book means so much to us," explains Ahmad. "It's our compass, in a way . . ."

Such is life in Daraya. Contrary to the narrative disseminated by Damascus, the city's so-called religious zealots have made identity-building their new religion. This deeply personal process belies the regime's narrative of bloodthirsty desperadoes being exploited by Islamic extremists. But how did an American self-help book end up on their list of favorites?

"Ustez told us about it," answers Ahmad.

Ustez, Daraya's veteran of civil disobedience. Clearly, this tireless professor has plenty of resources to share with his students.

"The first time he read it," continues Ahmad, "was when he was in prison in Sednaya. What a revelation! He made it his handbook, to guard against giving up inside that hostile environment. He adopted the philosophy of *7 Habits*, which he was intent on sharing with us."

From one jail to another. And now, inspired by their mentor's experience, Daraya's young dissidents in the shadows are applying this manual to their own needs. In the West, people skim Covey's book in search of effective solutions to temporary crises: a divorce, a breakup, a lay-off. Simple words for common problems. In Daraya, as in prison, readers are seeking not an easy, ready-made answer, but rather the keys to surviving in an extreme environment. This book is the psychologist they don't have, a reassuring companion in the worst moments of uncertainty. A crucial remedy for the sense of precariousness brought by violence, but also for the conflicts that can result from cohabitation in a confined space: arguments, jealousy, political disagree-ments, etc.

"It helped me get my ideas together. It also taught me how to live in a group, how to accept others and their dif-ferences, and how to maintain a climate of healthy compe-tition among us all."

At first Ahmad was happy enough relying on Ustez's summary of the book, which wasn't among those un-earthed from the rubble. When he wanted to read the whole thing, he turned to the internet, despite a poor con-nection. After a little digging through Google, the PDF of *7 Habits* popped up on Ahmad's screen. He then had to download and print it. But in Daraya, cut off from the world, paper is yet another rare resource that must be used sparingly. So Ahmad got the idea to print four pages on one. Columns of tiny writing, squeezed together like sardines, were bound like the secret pamphlets that circulated before the revolution.

"Even though you have to squint to read it, everybody fights over the book. We eventually made a second copy to keep up with the demand. It also inspired two lecture series: first inside the library, and then in the new underground debate space. Yasser al-Aiti, a well-known Syrian scholar in exile, gave a presentation about it from Istanbul, via Skype. The book's a real phenomenon," says Ahmad.

Dog-eared, ripped, and discolored, the book is passed endlessly from hand to hand. It's read, reread, brandished like a totem. In the particularly deadly winter of 2016, this self-help guide brings a sense of normality to Daraya's remaining inhabitants, who are still clinging to the hope that the conflict, which has been going on for five years, will in fact end one day. *7 Habits* offer its readers a way to view the conflict as temporary. It helps them to create distance from the helicopters dropping bombs and the daily confrontation with death, but also to quiet the impatience of fighters who hadn't anticipated the siege lasting so long. Most important, the book's easy-to-digest approach is a therapeutic outlet when the incessant rumbling of war makes it impossible for them to focus on works of literature and political thought.

On February 27, 2016, Daraya awakens to shocking silence. Not a single streak of powder in the sky, not a shot, not even the whine of a siren or the whirring of a helicopter. A sudden, almost troubling calm envelops the besieged enclave. Rumors, confirmed after a few hours, suggest a cease-fire: following intense negotiations, Washington and Moscow have finally brokered a truce between pro- and anti-Assad forces throughout Syria. The bombs have gone quiet. The war is placed in parentheses, at least temporarily. Could this be a new page for Daraya?

With the truce, a semblance of life returns to this underground stronghold. Like weeds growing amid the ruins, the remaining inhabitants begin to venture out. One, two, three, then a thousand . . . Eyes squinting, skin pale, drunk with exhaustion, they breathe in the fresh air and the silence, and absorb the natural light. At the other end of the line, Ahmad is smiling again. He cheerfully gives details of daily life without bombs.

Apart from a few unauthorized rounds of artillery

fire, the city has reclaimed some calm. Ahmad tells me about the people gathering at intersections in small groups, the tongues loosening, the resurrection of old slogans. He fills my inbox with new photos. In one, a young man brandishes a sign written in Arabic: "I wish I were a candle in the dark," from a poem by the Palestinian writer Fayeq Oweis. In another, a young woman veiled in white holds a piece of cardboard that reads: "I am neither al-Nusra Front nor Daesh. I'm just a girl enduring the siege of Daraya." A mix of made-up rhymes and mocking political slogans, these many signs celebrate the return of the word "freedom." "There's a feeling of revolution, like at the beginning," says Ahmad. A stirring identical to what he felt that first day.

Above their heads, the blue sky has been bleached by a powerful sun. As if spring has come early, impatient to bloom. Every image I receive shows small signs of rediscovered joy. Kids climb the skeleton of a dismantled swing set. Teenagers invade a forsaken square. A cat wanders. A bird perches atop a ripped-out cable. Ahmad tells me that visits to the library have resumed their peak rhythm. That books are again skipping from hand to hand. That after long months of interruption, the city's three schools have reopened their doors. Inside classrooms, children are reading and writing again, boys are roughhousing, and girls are creating bracelets from whatever scraps they find. It's still cold, but hearts are warmed by the return to an ordinary, reassuring commotion. They're warmed by laughter. By the desire to learn, to keep going. Quite simply, to exist. I listen to him and imagine little hands being raised in the air, the teacher trying to impose silence, questions spurting out, echoing back from pocked walls. 2 + 2 equaling 4, not 5.

Women, the invisible residents of Daraya, finally reappear in the streets. Shadows escaping the darkness, they once again emerge from their shelters. Going outside is no longer a risk. Amid the newfound quiet, free of the screams of metal, they resume the threads of trivial conversations, woven from the tiny woes that make up life. Gone are the sleepless nights, the inconsolable crying of panicked girls and boys, the terror of falling asleep and never waking. Milk again flows from the breasts of young mothers who had been unable to breastfeed beneath the bombs. Pushing old rusty strollers, the most emboldened among them show off their infants like trophies. Some six hundred babies have come into the world since the siege began. Born underground in most cases, they are experiencing the light of day for the first time. They cry, scream, gurgle. It's said that truth comes from the mouths of babes: What better way than this babbling to contradict the regime's insistence that there are no civilians left in Daraya?

After months of hell, the rebels can hold their heads high. They excavate their dreams. They sketch big projects—life, marriage, career. Always precise in his narration, Ahmad wants to give me updates about everybody. Ustez, the Professor, took advantage of this unimagined respite to launch a new seminar on marital relations for those daring, finally, to think about an engagement or wedding. Following a brief hiatus, Omar returned to his library. He reads there even more often and also gives new lectures. They feel a thirst to learn and share down to the bone. There is also a desire to let loose. Amid the ruins, a soccer pitch emerges. Quickly, holes are filled in, mounds of dirt are flattened, rubble is swept away. Eight teams of ten players are formed. Each group includes both fighters and activists. They play friendly matches in T-shirts before a public of curious spectators sitting on improvised bleachers. Suddenly, it's a time of unlimited possibilities. Even the grammar has changed. The inhabitants of Daraya are using the future tense, instead of speaking in hypotheticals. Living in the present has meaning again.

The walls are coming back to life, too. Down this street, or along that disemboweled sidewalk, sometimes at the base of a jagged wall, blooms a trail of poems, a constellation of drawings, a shield made of words . . . Abu Malek al-Shami, the group's tagger, roams the city with paint cans, covering it with color. On a wall deformed by a blast, he's drawn a four- or five-year-old girl in a blue-and-yellow dress. Standing on a hill made of skulls, she's writing the English word "hope" in capital letters with one chubby hand. This larger-than-life drawing is a lesson in optimism. It immortalizes these protesters as they thumb their noses at the war.

Another mural drawing, this one in chalk, grabs my attention. I am looking at a photograph taken by Ahmad, of a classroom with shattered windows in which the carcasses of desks jostle for room with metallic chair skeletons. In the back is a blackboard on which Abu Malek al-Shami has written something in Arabic, right to left: "We used to joke around and say, I hope the school falls down. And now it has fallen." Self-deprecation, another protective shell. My gaze shifts farther left, to the drawing: a boy in raggedy clothes and bare feet, wearing a backpack, scrawling "Daraya" in bloodred letters. I think of another activist–graffiti artist Ahmad recently told me about—Madjd Mohadamani, killed on February 19, 2016, by a shell shot from an army tank. And I also think, inevitably, about those teenagers in Daraa whose arrest for spraying anti-Assad graffiti triggered the 2011 uprising.

This mural is a way to pay them homage. It also declares: "We are still standing."

Saturday, March 19, 2016. I've just returned from a reporting assignment in Izmir, the coastal Turkish town that is the departure point for boats of Syrian refugees, so many of which capsize on their way to Europe. Hundreds of dead buried beneath the waves. Another consequence, terrible and invisible, of the war. My daughter, who's four, is waiting for me in Istanbul, her little arms stretched toward my heart. But that heart is heavy. So many children her age lie at the bottom of the sea. As usual, she wants to know everything about my reporting trip. For a four-year-old, life is a litany of questions. Scrolling through my phone, I show her life vests adorned with cute Hello Kitty faces. These are sold for children heading on the dangerous clandestine crossing toward Greece. I refrain from saying anything about shipwrecks or death. I just show Samarra her favorite little cat and she reminds me that it's Saturday, and that at 11:00 a.m., it's story time at the French Institute. A precious, never-to-be-missed ritual shared by mother and daughter. We put on our boots and jackets—the forecast says rain—before going down the stairs. Her hand in mine, we stride down the streets leading to Taksim. As we cross the packed square, we walk by the *simit* seller, near the old red tramway. French tourists are taking selfies. A lost Iranian visitor is trying to find his way. Some Saudis are hailing a taxi. On the other side, where Istiklal Avenue begins, a Syrian beggar sings to earn a few coins. Pigeons peck the bread crumbs at his feet.

It's 10:57. In three minutes, the story will begin. At the start of Istiklal Avenue, I walk up the steps to the French Institute. Behind me, Samarra's little voice chirps, "What a great day!" At the top of the stairs, I hand my bag to the security guard. He doesn't have time to open it. The air splits. A howling of metal. Violent. Intrusive. I turn around, stunned. Istiklal Avenue is a wave of panic. People rush headlong toward Taksim. A crazed flock. The explosion was so close. Unexpected. Thirty feet away— maybe less? I don't move, Samarra huddled against me. The guard pushes us inside. The doors close behind us. Outside, a torrent of noise. An uproar of worry and incomprehension. Chaos on the cobblestones.

Samarra pulls on my sleeve. "What was that?" Reassure her, at all costs. Skirt the question. Think of life, of those who were saved. Cling to the word "hope," like the one tagged on Daraya's faraway wall. Say something about fireworks. Remind her that it's 11:00 a.m., story time. Take her little hand. Cross the garden that leads to the library. Walk down the stairs. Push open the glass door. Down here, no one heard the explosion. The books formed a barricade. A paper shield. It's 11:05 and I whisper what just happened to Julie, the storyteller, slipping in the word "bomb." She frowns. Stands up straight. Claps her hands. "Come on! We're going to start the story." Her composure is inspiring. Sitting in a row on the bench, the children go silent. It's story time, and today, we have the story of Alfred, the dog who stinks. It's story time, and, outside, ambulances race by. It's story time, and Alfred is a hungry dog who can't get his fill of bones. It's story time and news updates flash on my phone. Confirmed attack. A suicide bomber. At least four dead. Dozens are injured. Daesh is named. Alfred barks. Sirens are shrieking. Julie reads. Helicopters are whirring. Julie turns the page. Children laugh. Alfred is a magical dog that brightens faces. Behind the wall of books, Istanbul is bleeding, struck at its heart. The sunny stars of fiction versus the fiery sparks of reality.

It's 11:45 and the story is almost over. And after? An insistent voice is telling me not to go back upstairs, to prolong this serene interlude for as long as possible, to stay underground and listen to other stories. About dogs. Cats. Snails. Bugs. To gorge myself on paper. To read everything within arm's reach. Until night comes, if that's what it takes. Is there someone outside who can turn off the sirens? Stop the police from using bullhorns? Tell my editor in chief that this time the reporting can wait? It's too early to leave. To confront the children with reality. To take away their right to dream—to hope! Books as a security blanket. The guard has other priorities. He has been told to evacuate the library. ASAP. Follow me. Proceed along the wall. In single file. Walk to the end of the garden. Go out the back door. Come on, faster. And good luck!

It's noon. Apart from a few panicked seagulls, Taksim Square is a desert. In my arms, Samarra whispers, "I think that's the first time I heard an explosion." How do I respond? I say nothing. The hum of helicopters would have eaten up my reply, anyway. Next, she asks me why they're roaming the sky. "Because of the storm . . . You remember, this morning, when you put on your boots?" It's the first lie that comes to mind. After all, it is story time.

Back home, I have a wild urge to call the book collectors. Ahmad, Shadi, Abu el-Ezz, Omar. To tell them about experiencing this mix of imminent death, the comfort of books, a retreat into fiction, the refuge of paper around me. To tell them what they already know, what they've been living every day, every hour, every minute for three years now. What's the point? The attack on Istiklal is just a tiny headline compared to the hell of Daraya. Then again, it has brought their world closer to me.

Two weeks later, on April 5, I receive a new email from Daraya. It's a group letter. A distress call signed by forty-seven women.

> We are women in the besieged town of Daraya and we are writing to you with an urgent call to save our town.
>
> The Syrian tragedy continues along with its repetitive scenes of violence and siege. Our town has witnessed the worst of bombing and destruction and cruel siege for over three consecutive years. Civilians have had to pay the price under the policy of starvation.
>
> The area is witnessing a shortage of all of the basic necessities, from the very simple, such as table salt, to the more complex, such as the ability to communicate with others. This has gotten much worse since Daraya was cut off from the neighboring town of Moadamiyet Al Sham [Moadamiya]. The town was closed off completely in the face of

fleeing civilians. We were left with a population of 8,000. There was no life outside of the basements because of the fear of being bombed. After the recent cessation of hostilities, calm returned to the town. Still, there is no life outside of the basements because all the buildings have been brutally destroyed. We're appealing to all who see this, near and far: we need immediate assistance.

There is no food at all in Daraya. There are cases of malnutrition and we have resorted to cooking soups made purely of spices in order to stave off hunger. There are signatories to this letter that have not eaten for at least two days—some longer. There is no baby milk and no breast milk due to malnutrition. Even something as simple but as necessary as dishwashing liquid is unavailable. There are no cleaning supplies in order for us to ensure hygiene and keep diseases away.

We the women of Daraya call for:

—An immediate lifting of the siege from all sides of the town

—The opening of the roads and the entry of basic necessities, from food and medicine to drinking water, clothes, shoes, and cleaning supplies

We call on the United Nations and all humanitarian and relief organizations to enter the town immediately and deliver humanitarian aid to all those affected as quickly as possible.

We appeal to journalists to write about Daraya

and shed attention on the plight of our town before mass starvation takes. We are on the verge of witnessing deaths from starvation. The infants and the elderly will be the first to succumb. Please take action before it is too late.

One by one, I read the signatures at the end of the letter: Sawsan, Khadija, Azizah, Mouna, Ikram, Samar, Najaa, Amal, Malak, Amani, Kinaz, Samera, Rama, Haifa, Fatemah, Maha, Merzat, Nour, Joumana, Afraa, Ghada, Khouloud, Wardah, Loubna, Amenah, Ayat . . . a string of names written as if in blood, a desperate SOS thrown at the world.

This is the first time, I think, that the "invisible" have broken their silence and abandoned their anonymity, at the risk of ending up on one of the regime's blacklists.

I can't even imagine the extent of the despair that would drive them to break from their traditional restraint.

Their letter is an act of self-exposure; it has no aim to please, seduce, or manipulate.

I know nothing about them. I can't see them. But I hear them. I can imagine them. Housewives, teachers, midwives, activists. I imagine their daily distress. I imagine their exhaustion, the miscarriages, the premature babies, the lack of sanitary napkins. I imagine the pee-stained beds of panicked children, the insomnia of anxious mothers, the tears in the dark. All hardships that aren't talked about, that are muffled by war, deferring to the bravery of the fighters. But behind the courage of men can be found the suffering of women.

Every war has its hidden female universe. A few days after receiving this collective letter, I meet online Hussam Ayash, another pillar of the Daraya group. Using his perfect English, which he learned through books, he oversees communication for the city council, sending reports and statements, translating letters, and answering questions from foreign journalists. Inside my Skype window, Hussam looks lost in his blue Adidas T-shirt. "I've lost forty pounds in three years," he says softly. At the age of thirty-two, standing five feet, nine inches tall, he weighs only 135 pounds. And yet, below eyes hollowed by fatigue and hunger, his triumphant smile lights up the screen.

"On really desperate days, I focus on the future," he enthusiastically tells me.

His future is named Zeina, a young Syrian from the suburb of Moadamiya, now a refugee in Istanbul. When he met her in late 2015, shortly before Daraya was surrounded, it was love at first sight. After a few weeks, halfway between the two rebel enclaves, the couple became engaged. They promised to support each other, but every attempted reunion was a dangerous undertaking. Hussam had to sneak into Moadamiya. He had to brave the threat of cannon fire from Assad's soldiers watching, from their hill, the clandestine comings and goings between the neighboring cities. Zeina would wait for him on the other side, heart racing, beneath her veil. A furtive face-to-face, long enough to chastely shake hands or exchange a few sweet nothings. That's it. The shortages in Daraya deprived Hussam of the pleasure of offering even the smallest present to his intended. "We established a rule between us: no gifts!" explains Hussam. But at their third meeting, Zeina broke the pact.

"She surprised me with two books," says Hussam.

Across the screen, he holds up one of them like a treasure: *Psychology and You*, coauthored by Julia C. Berryman et al. A prophetic gift?

"It was the night before they closed the last crossing between the two cities," Hussam recalls perfectly. "And also the night before Zeina left for Turkey, where her parents pressured her to follow them, though she didn't want to."

Since that hasty departure, the two have yet to see each other. But the book has stayed with Hussam. A proof of love. A vital comfort in the heart of this endless war. The catalyst, as well, of an epistolary relationship that has always revolved around reading.

"Books have become our common denominator. When we can't reach each other, each of us will read something. Then, as soon as we're able to connect on Skype or WhatsApp, we swap reading notes. Books bring us closer together. They're a bridge between us."

The two young lovers know so little about each other. And they're actually very different, including their literary tastes.

"Zeina's a fan of mushy romance novels. She's obsessed with them! But I'm more drawn to self-help books."

And yet they share a mad desire to love each other, urgently, to flirt with the unknown. To project themselves into a future that, though uncertain, is filled with shared dreams. On the advice of Ustez, Hussam devoured *Men Are from Mars, Women Are from Venus*, borrowed from the library, and he quickly encouraged his beloved to read it.

"It helped us, both of us, understand our differences, and manage the complexity of our long-distance relationship."

But they also have to adapt to the worries generated by war. Especially Zeina, whose exile in Turkey has only increased her anxiety.

"I realize that war is harder on the person who's far away. For me, the war is part of my daily life. It is my daily life. I chose it and accepted it. To be honest, I've lost any sense of fear."

Silence hovers after his last syllable, which is immediately replaced by hysterical laughter whose echoes reach all the way to my office walls. I watch him. Hussam is roaring with laugher. He's laughing with the ardor of someone desperately clinging to life. Who's proudly turning his back on death. What is really striking is how easily he steps back from the difficulties of what he's living through. How he accepts the absurdity of his situation, mocking it if he has to. When I tell him that he has the maturity of a wise old man, he answers me, detached: "Oh, you know, I was born in 1984, like George Orwell's novel. My life was doomed never to be simple! In four years, I've aged at least forty . . ."

Hussam takes another pause. I stare at him. Lined with subtle wrinkles, his face is a page of history. Four years during which he's lived through so much: the first revolutionary spasms; prison for refusing to shoot at protesters during his military service; the sarin gas attack, halfway through the summer of 2013, which almost cost him his life. Even his nom de guerre is a story in itself: he borrowed it from Hussam Ayash, the first martyr from Daraa, the famous city where the 2011 uprising began. (Many of the Daraya revolutionaries have adopted aliases during the siege for safety reasons, e.g., protecting family members living in regime-controlled areas.)

"Sometimes," Hussam continues, "I feel like I've gone

numb. Thankfully, Zeina's here to remind me what's normal."

Zeina, his virtual muse. His humanity, helping him keep his feet on the ground when the war tries to devour his emotions. She's his second half, the tears he no longer sheds, the fragility on worry-filled days when, at the other end of an unreliable connection, she whispers that she loves him. That she cares about him. That she'll wait for him until the end of time, despite their fights and disagreements.

"If I don't call her regularly, it's big trouble!" he laughs. "Zeina helps me stay anchored in what's real. And when we can't reach each other, books do the rest. They make me feel like I'm again the student I used to be, that I look like any other young man somewhere in the world. They take me away, for a moment, from my mess of a life."

In a city where the women remain invisible, a digital romance helps him endure the conflict. His love for Zeina gives him a goal. An objective that takes form beyond the front. The dream of a shared life, on the other side of the wall of war.

"Hey, how are you?"

"Hi, Ahmad. Any news?"

"Yes! Guess what? A United Nations and Red Crescent humanitarian convoy is finally coming to Daraya!"

"Really?"

"They'll be here any minute. A matter of days . . . or hours . . ."

"That's great news! Daraya's calls for help have finally been heard!"

"Yes, except they just told us that there won't be any food in the convoy. Only health kits, contraceptives. They're also sending glucose test patches . . . when what we actually need is sugar!"

It's May 11, 2016. This exchange on WhatsApp is only the starting point for a series of fiascos that will accelerate Daraya's descent into hell. A little over twenty-four hours later, the first humanitarian convoy in three and a half years finally approaches the enclave. At the end of interminable negotiations, the regime gave the green light on

certain conditions, notably no food—except for baby formula. But on the spot, the soldiers impose their own rules:
only vaccines will be allowed. The United Nations refuses
these unfair terms.

A few minutes later, at around 9:00 p.m. on May 12,
this black farce takes an even more tragic turn: nine artillery shells strike the spot where Daraya's residents had
gathered to wait for the convoy.

"Instead of long-awaited supplies, we got mortars!"
rails Ahmad.

The attack is deadly: it takes the lives of a father and
his son. Betrayed until their final breath. Killed for daring
to dream of filling their bellies.

A few days later, Ahmad bounces back. The cruelty
inflicted on his city, as tragic as it is absurd, inspires him
to film a short video that he emails me on May 16. I open
the file. A group of kids, barely older than the little girl
in Abu Malek's painting, are kneading mud on a mattress
serving as a table. You can hear Ahmad's voice behind the
camera: "What are you making?"

A girl responds, "A cake!"

"And how are you going to bake it?" continues Ahmad.

"Oh, by letting it dry in the sun!" explains another.

Then the children spread the mixture in pie tins with
their small hands, and decorate it with plastic flowers.

Since they don't have flour, they've made "works of art" to make fun of their misfortune.

Surprised by my surprise, Ahmad says, categorically, "Do you know why we're so creative? We have to find a way to convey our message to the international community, so they finally listen to us. Though if it was all up to me, I'd just sleep for a week straight."

But rest is a nonnegotiable luxury. Prevented from eating, the inhabitants of Daraya aren't allowed to sleep, either. Two weeks later, at the end of May 2016, the truce falls apart. The sky above the "many houses" of the devastated city rages anew. A deluge of death-dealing barrel bombs rips apart the sky. Helicopters are once again running furious, unleashing their iron cargos, arrogant blades menacing all corners of the city. "Assad wants to drive us mad," fumes Ahmad. After several failed attempts, I'm finally able to reach him on Skype. Exhaustion has etched bluish circles around his eyes. With the resumption of bombing, he is no longer sleeping. I've never seen him so worn out. Between explosions, he describes the horror to me, live. People buried beneath the rubble, volunteer aid workers overwhelmed with injured victims who need to be treated rapidly, lack of anesthetic. A feeling of déjà vu. The nightmare repeating. But worse.

Ahmad sends me photos of the cemetery. In the visibly

expanding square of martyrs, burials occur in an assembly line. No farewell prayers or tombstones. Simple mounds of dirt serve as graves. Pieces of cardboard bear the names of the deceased in place of tombstones. The city's run out of shrouds. Now they're fashioned from sheets, curtains, and tablecloths. "Sometimes, we bury the bodies but don't have time to wrap them in cloth," adds Ahmad.

In Daraya, now 90 percent destroyed, they're not even allowed a dignified death.

As the city plunges back into hell, the shortages spread. Deprived of running water and electricity since 2012, the inhabitants have run out of everything else: gas, food, toilet paper.

Even plastic bags and containers, which they had taken to burning to make fuel oil, have become scarce. To further starve the population, the regime has gone so far as to firebomb the surrounding fields.

"The children born under the siege don't even know what an apple looks like," reports Ahmad.

He breaks off. A dead silence. Then he grimly recounts the cases of malnutrition, the children who have stopped growing, the fear of a humanitarian disaster. His martyred suburb risks seeing the same fate as was inflicted on Madaya. Some thirty people in that city, also surrounded by government forces, died of hunger in 2015. Hidden from the cameras, seventeen other enclaves are scraping by under similar conditions: fifteen are under siege by the regime, and two others by the Islamist rebels of the al-Nusra Front. Hunger is a weapon of war. A particularly effective weapon. It can't be seen. But it slowly eats away at bodies. A destructive strategy perfectly calculated to control men through their stomachs.

On June 1, 2016, the first delivery of humanitarian aid finally reaches Daraya.

"It's about time!" writes Ahmad in a short message.

The joy is short-lived. Instead of long-awaited food supplies, the five trucks brought boxes of shampoo and mosquito nets, as well as a few wheelchairs, medicine, and baby formula. To the people's great dismay. The incident deals a final blow to the United Nations' reputation. Accused of doing nothing against a government disinclined to cooperate, it has lost the little credibility it had.

Since this latest fiasco, Ahmad has stopped waiting. He looks at life as it is, with no illusions whatsoever.

"We can only count on ourselves. The entire world has abandoned us," he says.

How do you survive in a world of absurdity? How do you ward off hunger? Avoid succumbing to anxiety and exhaustion? Defy violence when it creeps into every corner of existence? Ahmad tells me that everyone in Daraya has invented their own survival mechanisms. Between bombings, Hussam studies relentlessly, nose glued to his computer and eyes fixed on an uncertain future. He recently enrolled at the virtual Roshd University, which offers remote courses. Shadi runs after the bombs: he insists on filming everything, documenting everything, obsessed by the need to archive, as they happen, the crimes committed by the regime. If he dies, he tells himself, at least some traces will remain. He and his partners on the local council have drawn a detailed map of the cemetery of martyrs, so they can identify every grave site in case it is bombed. The war has taught them to think of everything.

And the library? It's still there, confined to its modest

basement, with its rows of books, overhead projector, and flower-patterned couches, intermittently open to the public. But there's a big hole since Omar left to take his place at the front line full-time. Out there, anti-Assad soldiers have endured enormous losses and ammunition is starting to run out. It's impossible to escape the combat zone, even for a minute. And yet Omar remains faithful to his books, preferring the company of Ibn Khaldun and Nizar Qabbani during his very rare breaks with a cup of boiling-hot tea. He's got to be one of the last Daraya residents to have not given up on political essays. The other readers lack concentration. Enthusiasm. Even self-help books, once so popular, are no longer sought-after.

Ahmad confides in me that, in these moments of endless distress, his only solace comes in reading accounts by people who have lived through similar experiences. He and his friends discovered a few books about the siege of Sarajevo on the library shelves. Too young to be aware at the time of the blockade imposed by the Serbian army on the capital of Bosnia and Herzegovina, from 1992 to 1996, they belatedly discovered this history, eyes wide open. Four years of incessant bombings, of hunger, of terror imposed on 350,000 inhabitants trapped in a hellish valley. Four years of blind violence that cost the lives of more than 11,500 people and splintered the city into a thousand pieces. Destroyed buildings. Gutted monuments. Including the grand library, where more than a million and a half volumes went up in smoke. Attacked by a rain of shrapnel, it was the foundation of Sarajevo's cultural heritage. The people of Daraya are face-to-face with history itself. Like a mirror of their own history. Their tragedy, their pain. Their courage and their fight for freedom.

"Reading about Sarajevo is a way to feel less alone. To tell ourselves that others, before us, lived through the same thing. In another country. Another context. But thanks to their accounts, I feel less vulnerable. I find an inner strength that pushes me forward," says Ahmad.

Atop the memories etched in these books come the words of a living collective memory. With the help of the re-nowned American war reporter Janine di Giovanni, who had covered both the Bosnian and Syrian wars, Ustez established a direct link to the survivors of the Sarajevo blockade. In the course of their exchanges, a WhatsApp group specially created for him gives rise to a survival tip here, an anecdote there, and even a pledge of support when the entire world seems to have already turned the page on Daraya.

But for Ahmad, the greatest comfort goes by the name of Mahmoud Darwish. Among the works by this Palestinian poet, who died in 2008 and is idolized in the Arab world, Ahmad knew his poems about the siege of

Beirut, in 1982, and the siege of Ramallah, in 2002. Before the revolution, he had dismissed these texts on more than one occasion, remote as they were from his concerns. Since the siege has intensified, these two literary masterpieces have taken on greater meaning, prompting him to memorize entire passages. Every morning, he listens in a loop to the audio track recorded by the poet that one of his friends dug up on YouTube.

"I listen to these poems like you'd listen to a secret voice whispering things you're unable to express. The way someone sings what you're incapable of singing. I find myself in every word, in every line. I identify with the experiences lived, the waiting beneath the shells, the time that becomes space, the martyrs that you're unable to forget. I listen to the verses and think: that's exactly how I feel!"

Ahmad breaks off. His elation comes through the screen, floating above my desk. He tells me that if he had to choose between these two poetry collections by Mahmoud Darwish, his favorite remains the more recent one, *State of Siege*, which describes Ramallah when the Israeli army imposed a blockade on the Palestinian city. I ask him if he has a favorite part.

"The beginning, of course," he responds.

And with a voice charged with emotion, he begins to read.

Here on a hill slope facing the sunset and the
  wide-gaping
gun barrel of time
near orchards of severed shadows
we do as prisoners and the unemployed do:
we nurse hope.*

Ahmad slowly lifts his head toward the screen, his lips frozen in a pained smile. Everything's been said, set in writing in beautiful lines that defy the attrition of time and war. Writing that is alive, precise. The words that echo in this poem speak for him. For Daraya.

---

* Mahmoud Darwish, *State of Siege*, trans. Munir Akash and Daniel Abdal-hayy Moore (Syracuse, NY: Syracuse University Press, 2010), 3.

Hope, despite everything. Hope grown in a makeshift vegetable garden in the corner of a courtyard. Hope in the sunflowers breaking free of the dry and polluted earth. Hope in a shrub planted in a crater left by a shell. I go over a new series of images sent by my correspondents in Daraya. They are poetry incarnated, showing exceptional ingenuity and that "inner strength" described by Ahmad that helps them resist. To avoid starving to death, the city's residents have transformed their courtyards into plots in which they grow the ingredients of their modest daily meals: lettuce, spinach, tomatoes, potatoes. Along with bulgur wheat, taken from the city's last reserves, these few vegetables are the foundation of their diet. Sometimes, when the harvest is bad, they have to make do with a simple soup of boiled tree leaves and roots simmered in a pot.

"It's disgusting!" says Hussam on Skype, making a face.

I recognize his mischievous smile, a strategic shield

against the horrors of daily life. Since he confided in me about Zeina, we've been talking a lot on WhatsApp. In perfect English, he tells me about his strong feelings for her, their lovers' quarrels, the questions he asks himself afterward. A stranger's ear undoubtedly offers him the perspective he needs. Before every conversation, I'm careful to push away my cup of coffee, to move the box of cookies out of the eyeline of my webcam. But this time, he's the one who insists we talk "cuisine." A way to curb his cravings, he says.

"The meal that I miss the most? Grilled chicken!" He chuckles.

He elaborates down to the smallest detail: the crackling of the skin, the sauce softening the legs and thighs, the distinct flavor of the drumstick . . .

"In fact, speaking of hunger, it's lunchtime." Hussam maintains the routine, with his now familiar inclination to chase away the thick dust of dark memories.

He stands up. His head is out of the frame, revealing legs as thin as baguettes. The young man pivots his laptop for a tour of his modest living room. With one hand, he indicates his couch and a shelf covered in papers. The image freezes, snagged by a bad connection, before landing on a gas stove. I cast a curious glance at the pans and dishes piling up in the sink. I feel like I'm actually in his kitchen.

"May I invite you to share my meal?" he continues, in a joking tone.

On the shelf, next to boxes emptied of all food, a simple bag of bulgur.

"My daily feast!" he laughs, putting water on to boil.

Hussam has made this his meal for weeks, once a day, relying on modest reserves to hold out another few months.

"Bon appétit," I answer ironically.

A vapor cloud has invaded his kitchen, speckling the computer screen with small white dots. Hussam disappears again, then reappears, his plate filled with a beige mush. Before he begins his meal, the taste buds in his memory come alive, prompting other culinary confessions.

"Sometimes, to fight our hunger, we all meet up at someone's place and spend the entire night talking about food. Everyone will say his favorite meal—Grandma's stuffed zucchinis, a meat broth, your favorite spices, the pistachio dessert you dream of finishing it off with."

Another tip, he says, is to linger over a bowl of soup, pretending to savor every spoonful, like a massive gourmet dinner relished until the last bite. Without bread, the exercise can only go so far. Up until 2013, the local council managed to keep the last bakery that hadn't been bombed in operation. And then, one day all the flour supplies were exhausted, so they had to go without. But survival, once again, depends on humor: trying to compensate for the absence of something so popular among Syrians, Hussam and his friends make jokes, taking turns poking fun at the poor customers, elsewhere in the world, who agonize over choosing between a baguette, a brioche, and a whole-wheat loaf.

"At least we're spared such concerns," says Hussam, smiling.

And then on the evening of June 9, 2016, the fourth day of the fasting month of Ramadan, hope, true hope, finally knocks on Daraya's door. This time, it crosses the blockade. Thanks to a minitruce lasting forty-eight hours, nine trucks enter the besieged city. They are filled with bags of flour, other dry goods, and medicine. The provisions are far from sufficient: it's barely enough to last one month. But for the suburb's roughly eight thousand starving inhabitants, it's already a miracle.

"Finally! We had stopped thinking it would happen," says Ahmad enthusiastically, sending real-time updates.

But the trap snaps closed as quickly as it was set. The next day, I learn from the news that regime planes are again raging in the sky, stopping the distribution of the long-awaited food supplies. There is a chorus of declarations of indignation from the international community, denouncing Damascus's duplicity. In vain. The bombs dropping from the sky don't care about words.

I call Ahmad, worried. How is he? Was he able to find

refuge in a relatively safe shelter? How is he holding up in this latest nightmare? At the end of the line, he's unable to speak. He's lost his voice. His throat is empty. I can tell that he is beaten, depressed. From all the time spent talking to him over the internet, I've learned to read between the lines, to anticipate his responses, to decipher his silences. This isn't a normal silence. For the first time, he's run out of words to talk about Daraya.

June 12, 2016. It's 5:00 a.m. and I can't sleep. I search the internet for the slightest sign of life from Daraya. Ahmad is no longer answering my calls. All my messages sent via WhatsApp remain unanswered. They haven't even been read: there is no ✓✓ signaling the messages have been received. I look through the list of my other contacts on my phone. Hussam, away. Shadi, away. Omar, away. A silence as blank as an empty page. I'm afraid I've lost them for good. Without the internet, the world has become vast again, increasing a distance we naively thought abolished. And to think that I had started to believe that our connection built over the Web offered them a pocket of safety. But now their distress calls are muted, their songs ignored; the entire planet is out of hearing range. The space between us and them has grown darker, swallowing their last words.

A few miles from Daraya, a graveyard city mottled by barrel and cluster bombs, propaganda-spouting loud-speakers promise to get rid of the "terrorists" once and for all. From up high in his palace, Assad the ophthalmologist dons even thicker blinders, hurrying soldiers to the gates of the rebel suburb so they can seize more territory. Far from the world's cameras, the noose tightens. Without witnesses, I imagine the worst. A major military offensive. A deadly attack. An invisible massacre, like Hama in 1982, when online social networks hadn't yet been created. I can't stop myself from thinking of Ahmad and his companions: victims twice over, first of the bombs and then of the international inertia that adds to their suffering.

Still no news from them, so I scan Facebook, WhatsApp, and YouTube in search of some trace, however minuscule. No pictures. Not one word. Amid this worrying blackout, I turn to their Instagram accounts. Ahmad's has been inactive for several months. The last photo he posted is heartbreaking: a mother in a white head scarf burying her son, yet another addition to Daraya's list of martyrs. I go backward, traveling through time, dissecting every shot, every detail, in the kaleidoscope of his daily life. I come across a photo of a red rose with the slogan "Make love, not war." I stop on one of a kitten in the arms of a fighter. I spot Ahmad, Hussam, and Shadi's boyish faces in a black-and-white selfie. They're posing in front of the city's ruins, the standard background for most of their shots. I recognize them again, this time in a photo, lounging on a living room rug. Viewing this companionable interlude amid chaos, I can't help but think about the absurdity of war. Or rather of the normalcy that creeps in despite everything.

And I think back to the secret library. To Omar's manuscripts. To Abu el-Ezz's injuries. To the hopeful chant of *"Jenna! Jenna!"* To the roses and water bottles handed to regime soldiers. To the impassioned gazes. To the pieces of cardboard calling for peace. To destroyed dreams in the making. It's hard for me to look away from these photos: the war has pinned the eyes of old men into the faces of these young rebels. I rewind the series of events. How did we get here? What monster snuck its way into Assad's brain? Into the minds of all those tyrants, big and small, namely in Russia and Iran, who insist on blindly supporting him? I can't imagine what might be said, one day, when they run Daraya's obituary. A city sacrificed out of thirst for power. A dream of democracy broken by the ravenous ambition of men. A tiny dot of hope wiped from the Syrian map. One more victim on the list of cities destroyed by siege: Madaya, Homs, East Aleppo, etc.

In my office in Istanbul, I turn in circles like a whirling dervish. I fill the silence by clinging to what connects me to Ahmad and his friends: books. I reread *The Alchemist, The Shell, Les Misérables, The 7 Habits*. I immerse myself in them one by one. I inhale these works with one long breath, like I'm free diving. Verses from Mahmoud

Darwish's *State of Siege* run along with my thoughts, a chorus:

> *The siege is a waiting game,*
> *time held suspended on a ladder*
> *leaning into the eye of a storm.*

Each time, I stumble over the same couplet:

> *Writing is a puppy snapping at nothingness,*
> *composing bloodless wounds.**

Why write? To what end? If only I could skip pages of this book in progress. Their book, Daraya's book. If only I could anticipate what happens next, hoping it will be less tragic, and after some happy event place the final period. If they are gone, does this text still have any meaning? Novels have an advantage over nonfiction: they venture onto the paths of imagination, bypassing the highway of reality. You make up a transition, an outcome, new characters. But switching to fiction at this stage strikes me as out of the question. The importance of this work lies precisely in recounting the fragility of the moment. To record it within the vastness of time and memory. To collect the

---

* Darwish, *State of Siege*, 49, 155.

traces—even slight and sometimes intimate—of this present that's disappearing at the speed of a bomb, too quickly condemned to the past: in personal accounts, in the pages of books read, in the lulls of war, in individual memories, in tears and laughter.

This book is a little of all that at once: the story, even unfinished, of these invisible heroes. I can't give up on it.

Write so as not to forget. So as not to forget *them*.

One month goes by, punctuated by worry, full of intro-spection. One month of trying to dig up new details, however minuscule, of compiling everything I've been able to gather up until now. Pictures, snippets of sentences cut short by bombs, fragments of life that have escaped the conflict.

And then, on July 12, my cell phone comes back to life. "Shadi's been hurt."

Alternating between relief and worry, I reread the message Ahmad sent by WhatsApp. Shadi's-been-hurt. Period. Then silence again. This damn waiting. Waiting on a ladder, leaning . . .

When the connection is restored at the end of the day, Shadi himself gives me an update. He's wearing a large bandage on his left hand and tries to be reassuring: he's out of danger. But he's still in shock from an attack that just occurred. The past few weeks have been hell. Regime soldiers are escalating their offensive at the city limits, try-ing to seize new plots of land. To outrun the danger, the rebels of Daraya have been changing shelters frequently, hunkering down in basements. Hence Shadi's limited access to his office (and the internet). The attacks stop and start, following a seemingly endless pattern: two days of intense bombing, then a day of respite. But this morning, July 12, looked to be more forgiving. Shadi finally ventured outside, accompanied by Malek, a buddy from the media center. They wanted to check in on some families, make a few videos, and evaluate the extent of the damage. Together, they decided on a neighborhood in the western part of town. A flash, then a rain of rocket fire cut off their path. The two friends were caught off guard, they wanted to turn back. Too late: a new volley landed right next to them. This time, the ground trembled beneath their feet. Impossible to take a step forward or backward. The smoke created a barrier. Dust mixed with cement powder. In shock, Shadi didn't realize right away that he'd been injured.

"I couldn't see anything anymore. I cried out, 'Malek! Malek!' I was scared that something had happened to him."

Shadi groped his way out. It was only once he found his friend that his left hand began to throb. He looked down—it was red with blood. Pieces of shrapnel had torn off bits of skin and dislocated his index and middle fingers. The pain was immediate. And excruciating. A van serving as an ambulance rushed him to a makeshift hospital, the only one left in town. The nurses there were overwhelmed. When the doctor finally arrived, he operated as quickly as possible.

"The morphine wasn't strong enough. I was screaming in pain. The doctor hummed a popular song with 'Shadi' in the title to encourage me."

Once again, Shadi had had a close brush with death—the rocket had landed less than twenty inches from where he was standing.

"A few more inches, and that would have been it for me."

I inquire about Ahmad, Hussam, and Omar. Were they with him? Are they safe? Shadi tries to reassure me. "We weren't together. The rest of the group is fine. We all change shelters constantly to avoid the strikes."

And his camera? As always, he'd been wearing it over his shoulder, close to his heart. Just out of surgery, he realized that the lens was broken, shattered by missile fragments. It was unusable. As for the body, it was completely scorched. It turns out that it acted as his bullet-proof vest.

"My camera saved my life."

Shadi stops talking. A contemplative silence. His indispensable camera worked up until the final "click"—and then it stood between him and death.

"Later on, I realized that the memory card was still intact, despite the damage to the camera. All the photos that I had taken before the attack were there. A miracle!"

These archived images are vital. An irrefutable mark of Syria's war—permanent, painful, and necessary.

On July 14, a new letter, this time signed by the local council, makes its way out of Daraya. The tone is serious and alarming. Addressed directly to French president François Hollande, it is a final distress call to the world.

Mr. President,

We, the residents of Daraya, currently fighting for our freedom, are writing to alert you to the threat hanging over our town. More than eight thousand inhabitants have been living under siege since 2012, right outside Damascus, in extremely difficult conditions. Electricity, water, and communications have been completely cut off. Over the past few weeks, this situation deteriorated dramatically as the regime bombings intensified, in flagrant violation of the cease-fire signed in Vienna in December 2015. The "humanitarian corridor" carved by revolutionary forces between Daraya and the neighboring suburb of Moadamiya has been destroyed, as have the city's farming fields, depriving the population of its remaining resources. The inhabitants who sought refuge in Daraya have been forced to hide out in the apartment buildings in ruins downtown.

In four years, more than eight thousand barrels of explosives have been dumped on the city. We fear that the recent advances by Assad's forces and their allies are merely the prelude to a major assault that will lead to the massacre of Daraya's remaining inhabitants and the total destruction of the cradle of Syrian pacifism. Daraya, which resisted both the regime and the extremists of Daesh, risks being subjected to a new massacre, like the one in August 2012, where loyalist forces killed more than 640 civilians in only two days. Everything happening now is the result of a strategic offensive, led by Bashar al-Assad and implemented with the logistical support of Moscow. Fighting and bombing stopped for two months after the cease-fire took effect on February 27, 2016. It should be noted that despite the regime's repeated violations of the truce, revolutionary forces have respected the agreement. They have always called for a political solution, as have the civilian bodies whose authority they acknowledge. Regime forces, however, completely abandoned the truce in the month of May. Since then, they have been advancing toward the center, where the remaining inhabitants are trapped.

Mr. President, in order to prevent pacifist Daraya

from becoming a Syrian Guernica, the countries who are part of the cease-fire task force must take responsibility. We are calling for an urgent intervention to force the regime to apply Security Council Resolution 2254 and the December 2015 Vienna deal. In addition to a cease-fire, we are calling for the establishment of a humanitarian corridor, the evacuation of victims and their protection, and, finally, the lifting of the blockade. France, which has always stood with the Syrian people, must use its influence to prevent a massacre in Daraya, for which it would bear responsibility, as would all those who sponsored the truce. Despite a tragic civilian and military situation, the city of Daraya will continue to resist and fight for a political, pacifist solution, as it has done for four years. However, today, only an intervention by the international community, by political and revolutionary forces, will prevent the total annihilation of Daraya and its inhabitants.

Long live revolution, dignity, and freedom.

Did this July 14 appeal have any chance to be read?

It's 11:33 p.m. in France. And this evening, François Hollande has other worries on his mind. In Nice, the traditional fireworks have just ended in blood: a truck acted as

a battering ram, drove into the crowd, and killed eighty-
six people—injuring dozens more. Another act of barbarism, claimed by Daesh.

I receive both pieces of news on my cell phone in the
middle of the night, with an uncustomary delay. The day
before, I crossed the Mediterranean, that seemingly peaceful sea whose waves have devoured countless migrants, and
landed on a Greek island. The connection here is terrible.
I have to sidle up to my neighbor's wall to get even the
weakest of Wi-Fi signals. I take a pillow onto the veranda
and lie under the stars. I draft a response to Ahmad. As fatigue adds to my feelings of powerlessness and guilt, words
push and shove in my mind. Assad is bombing Syria. The
Islamic State is killing in France and elsewhere. The world
is on fire and I'm on a Greek rock, isolated, lulled by the
singing of crickets. I had promised to bring my daughter, Samarra, here on a long vacation. I keep staring at
the blank screen on my computer. I'd like to tell Ahmad
that we won't forget them. Promise him that their letter
will wake up consciences. That there will be better days.
Grapes on the vines. Olives in the orchards. Bread in their
bellies. I'd like to tell them that in the twenty-first century,
this kind of tragedy can't go unpunished. That the French
Revolution didn't happen overnight, that it took time, that
the equation "liberty, equality, fraternity" still holds. That
one day, the little girl in the blue-and-yellow dress will no

longer have to stand on skulls to write the word "hope." That 2 and 2 does in fact make 4. That 5 will be condemned in the end by the United Nations Security Council. A crime against humanity, just like the bombings, the sarin gas attacks, the prison abuses and rapes, the siege of cities, and the torture by hunger.

I'd like to tell them all that.

But what will come tomorrow?

Will the United Nations deign to take action?

Will it be able to stop the killing machine?

Tomorrow, will their distress call be erased by other tragedies? Other threats? Other conflicts?

Tomorrow, once it's too late, will the international community finally wake up?

On July 29, I'm back in Istanbul and Ahmad sends me a message.

He's devastated. "Omar's been killed."

Omar. Daraya's Ibn Khaldun. The booklover. The most enthusiastic of the library's readers. The latest victim of this murderous siege. I dial Ahmad's number immediately. I want to convey my condolences. I know how much he cared for Omar—the hope of Daraya, the insatiable learner turned into a soldier by circumstance. The internet connection is choppy. I understand every other word. Using WhatsApp messages and brief Messenger chats, Ahmad walks me through the past few days. The constant barrage of aerial raids. The ground offensive against more neighborhoods. To the west. The south. Everywhere. The shrinking of residential zones. The recapture of the last farming plots. And the assault that had appeared imminent on the remaining food reserves. Omar and the rebels were undermanned and poorly equipped. Their simple Kalashnikovs against the regime's tanks and planes.

Little matter. They had to stop this attack. It would have been fatal for the city's inhabitants. So they went all in: they risked venturing beyond the usual defense lines to plant explosives on enemy territory. From high on their mountain, the Fourth Division soldiers spotted their maneuver. The cannons opened fire. Omar fell. He never stood back up.

And that day, for the first time in a long time, Ahmad cried.

"The news of his death came as a shock. I was paralyzed, my sadness insurmountable. Omar was an icon of this revolution. A fighter under duress who dreamt of peace and a future for Syria."

His voice changes, choked by sobs. I can feel his grief, the void created by the absence of his friend. Like a page of Daraya that's been ripped out. And I think, inevitably, of Omar as a young, atypical warrior, a gun-toting, book-loving poet, whom I met for the first time through an internet window in the fall of 2015. I think back to the PDFs flooding his cell phone. To his thirst to learn. To his stubborn taste for politics. To Machiavelli's *The Prince*, which I wanted to give him, and which he will never read. I think back to the front line, where books kept him company—his "mini library," as he called it. I imagine them scattered on the ground, lost amid dust and cannon powder. Were Ahmad and his friends able to salvage some of them, modest souvenirs in this war that erases everything? Were they able to give him a final farewell at the cemetery? To write his name on a cardboard grave marker? To whisper a few prayers?

"Sadly, none of that . . . In fact, it wasn't even possible for us to get back the bodies of Omar and the three other fighters killed alongside him. Regime soldiers took them away. They took the corpses hostage."

The kind of news story you hope never to write. Words that you struggle to put on paper. But you must, so people know the regime didn't just kill Omar and steal his youth. It humiliated him until the end, depriving him of a grave, of a final resting place among his own people.

The next day, I contact Ahmad again. I want to see how he's doing, assure myself that he's holding up. He hasn't slept at all. He and his friends, he says, stayed up all night. An evening of remembrance improvised in a modest apartment. For hours on end, they watched videos and remembered the books Omar loved so much. They reread certain passages to ease their sadness.

"The memory of him that sticks with me is someone who believed in our revolution until the end . . . He had loads of plans. He could have pursued a career in politics. He dreamt of getting married, of starting a family. He had even planned his engagement to a young woman from Damascus, once the war was over. Not long before he died, he enrolled, like Hussam, at Roshd University, the online school. He rubbed elbows with death every day but had an unshakable faith in life. He really inspired us!"

Ahmad breaks off, pensive. Memories are jostling in his head. Too many to sort. He's overwhelmed and apologizes for not being able to get his thoughts together. He gives me one final word, however, before he hangs up.

"He recently confided something in me. The revolution had interrupted his dream of becoming an engineer. But it opened an unexpected door for him—reading. That door led to writing, too. He wanted to pick up a pen one day and write for later generations. Write, yes, write for better tomorrows. A Syria for all Syrians. A utopia that he believed in."

But the door closed. And the pen was stilled before its time. Broken by war.

When I hung up that day, I thought of "A Sleeper in the Valley," the sonnet by Arthur Rimbaud, which I learned in my youth.

A green hole where a river sings;
Silver tatters tangling in the grass;

Sun shining down from a proud mountain:
A little valley bubbling with light.

A young soldier sleeps, lips apart, head bare,
Neck bathing in cool blue watercress,
Reclined in the grass beneath the clouds,
Pale in his green bed showered with light.

He sleeps with his feet in the gladiolas.
Smiling like a sick child, he naps:
Nature, cradle him in warmth: he's cold.

Sweet scents don't tickle his nose;
He sleeps in the sun, a hand on his motionless chest,
*Two red holes on his right side.**

Poems have a miraculous power to transcend eras. Rimbaud was sixteen when he composed these short verses. It was 1870, during the Franco-Prussian War. Another time. Another conflict. Other tragedies. If he had written them in the twenty-first century, I don't think they would have changed much. These verses speak for Daraya, railing against the death of a young fighter, lulled by the

---

* Arthur Rimbaud, *Rimbaud Complete*, ed. and trans. Wyatt Mason (New York: Modern Library, 2002), 37.

pulsing, calming song of Nature, on the path to the final sleep.

I read the sonnet to Asmaa, my Syrian friend and interpreter. Together, we translated it into Arabic, making the rhymes ring out even more than they do in French. I sent it to Ahmad, dedicating it to Omar, the sleeper of the Syrian valley.

Omar's death marks a radical turning point in the lives of Daraya's inhabitants. With this loss, they begin to realize that their city's days are numbered. And yet they're far from imagining that the worst is yet to come. On Thursday, August 4, regime helicopters surprise the city by sprinkling it with a new poison—napalm. In one day, a dozen incendiary bombs are dropped on apartment buildings, transforming their targets into massive fireballs. The blaze is devastating: it burns everything in its path. Walls. Buildings. Trees. Leaves intended for the daily soup . . . The landscape in ashes. Pieces of buildings up in smoke. Victims of a no-holds-barred demolition plan. A scorched-earth strategy, calculated and considered, reaches its climax.

After 1,350 days of siege, these citizens thought they had endured everything: barrel bombs, sarin gas, rockets, cannon fire. During 1,350 days of siege, Daraya was transformed into a vast field of ruins. Piles of rubble everywhere. Dried-out olive orchards. Scraps of life in the midst of death. And now Bashar al-Assad has condemned the city to an auto-da-fé, a public burning, ignoring the international ban on the use of napalm. A campaign of mass destruction to make Daraya yield, to erase it from the map of Syria.

My increasingly rare exchanges with Ahmad, Shadi, and Hussam are limited to the same questions, to which they respond with a few emojis:

"You okay?"

"☹"

"Hang in there!"

"☺"

Every once in a while I receive a few more images of Daraya, when the internet there starts working again. Once fertile fields rolled over by tanks. Burnt flower buds. Streets blackened with soot.

Above all, I tell myself, keep writing. Keep the gap open. Warn of the devastation. But the United Nations is paralyzed. Politicians are bogged down in security concerns. Everywhere, the specter of Daesh looms. Some leaders even see fit to renew ties with Damascus to fight this mutual enemy. And the moderate Syrian opposition in all this? Wake up, my poor friend, it hasn't existed for quite some time! Meanwhile, the hourglass is tilting in Bashar al-Assad's favor: hands free, scope set on Daraya, he lights the flames with total impunity. *Fahrenheit 451*, anyone?

Burning to obliterate. Burning to dehumanize. On August 16, in the middle of summer, the nightmare everyone dreaded becomes reality.

"The hospital's been attacked by napalm!"

This time, it's Hussam sounding the alert on WhatsApp. Helicopters have dumped their incendiary bombs on the city's last clinic. The attack left four wounded, who were immediately evacuated. The beginning of the end? Three days later, four barrels full of napalm are again dropped over what remains of the building housing the hospital. This time, the entire structure is consumed by flames. A skeleton burnt to ashes. Patients are transported at the last second to shelters out of danger. In dark holes, everyone becomes a nurse, psychologist, or simple lighting engineer, smartphone flashlights pointed at wounds. A desperate network of solidarity emerges. Parents take turns taking children out early in the morning, before the bombings start. Women hold back their tears as they hum nursery rhymes. Everyone performs their prayers far from the mosque, damaged several times over. Some civilians, who had stayed out of the fighting until now, even join the Free Syrian Army on the front line to defend Daraya from the Fourth Division tanks.

But the reality is inescapable: the city has been backed into a corner. Doomed to burn.

"We've run out of everything: food, fighters, weapons to defend ourselves," explains Hussam after a few days.

Wracked with fatigue and despair, Daraya is dying. For the first time since the siege began, this rebel stronghold initiates direct negotiations with the regime.

"Our priority is to save civilians. The local council and the Free Syrian Army have accepted the idea of a deal with the government. An evacuation plan is up for discussion. But talks are dragging on and we're not sure of anything . . ."

And what about him, Hussam, how is he holding up?

"Oh, well, I'm counting the days until I die," he says, laughing nervously.

Ahmad has become fatalistic as well, especially since Omar's death.

"We no longer bother distinguishing between day and night. We're in a daze, incapable of thinking. We spend most of our time underground, in the office at the media center. Death is everywhere, ready to claim us," he tells me.

They no longer expect anything from the United Nations, other than that it will come one day to collect their bones from the city's ruins. Unless, he says, they've already been burnt to ashes beneath the embers. Once again, humor, though increasingly dark, is essential to survival. In a new photo sent via WhatsApp, a mocking slogan reads: "We hope that the heat of the napalm over Daraya doesn't ruin the lovely weather for the United Nations delegations in Damascus!" The words are hard and bitter, but they stand strong, one next to the other, perfectly aligned from right to left on pieces of cardboard that serve as banners.

"Irony is basically our last rampart. When despair eats away at us, we tell each other jokes and turn to *shelli*," says Ahmad.

"*Shelli?*"

"Yeah, it's a popular expression, meaning superficial conversation, gossip, blah blah blah. It's reassuring, makes us feel normal. Like a safeguard . . ."

Shelli. The word lingers on my lips. A familiar taste. *Shelli* . . . When I hang up that night, I think of Mustafa Khalifa. *Al-Qawaqa'a. The Shell*. And I can't help but see a connection there, even if it's unconscious, with *shelli*. That famous protective shell, an armor against violence. A torrent of verbs and nouns hatching beneath the flames of war.

Augustus 27, 2016. 9:00 a.m. Like gunpowder smoke, the message that was inevitable after four years of blockade bursts onto my phone screen.

"We're leaving ☹"

It comes from Ahmad, who wrote it early in the morning as he hurriedly packed his bags. In the previous weeks, as their situation deteriorated, Asmaa and I had taken turns maintaining a minimum of contact with the young people of Daraya. Small, friendly words, blinking out to them like fireflies in the middle of the night, to assure them of our support, as limited and far-off as it may be. Then, three days ago, the enclave had woken to silence. No planes. No artillery fire. An unusual and frightful calm for 6:00 a.m. As if clearing the way for yet another tragedy. News spread that an envoy from the Fourth Division had issued an ultimatum to the city's inhabitants: leave Daraya immediately or end up buried alive there. The city leaders and the rebels unsuccessfully attempted to negotiate for the fighters to stay in Daraya, even without their weapons. Or be relocated to the city of Daraa, then still held by the opposition. At the end of tense talks, the dissidents felt they had no choice but to capitulate. The city had to surrender.

"There was nothing left to eat, nothing to protect ourselves with. The regime had burned all our farming land. It was leave or die . . . We had to save our families, at any cost," explains Ahmad, in a series of texts.

On August 26, the bitter truce took effect. Buses arrived at the city entrance to pick up the civilians first. Many were lugging old duffel bags in one hand, and leading one or two children with the other. Approximately seventy-five hundred men and women emerged from underground, faces waxen, some in rags, to cross the ruins of their ghost town one final time. Then, beneath the vengeful gazes of regime soldiers, they climbed aboard. Flanked by the Syrian Red Crescent, the buses drove them to the neighboring town of Sahnaya, a few miles to the south. This forced evacuation began four years to the day after regime soldiers killed hundreds in Daraya in August 2012.

On August 27, the seven hundred or so anti-Assad fighters remaining in Daraya follow, along with their families. Their destination is farther away: the government has decided to send them to Idlib, well in control of anti-Assad forces, 186 miles northwest. Thirty buses, heavily flanked, are waiting to bring them to a new unknown.

Through WhatsApp exchanges during their departure, alternating between written messages and voicemails, Ahmad explains to me that he, Hussam, and Shadi deliberately chose to go with this second convoy, rather than with the civilians.

"We wanted to make sure that the evacuation of civilians took place without any problems before we could leave. We didn't want their deaths on our consciences, especially not those of their children. They didn't ask to be here. But we stayed in Daraya by choice. It's on us to assume our responsibility until the end."

Their commitment is unfailing. For days, they've been expecting death to arrive, like they're in some hellish waiting room. Terrified as they are, their sense of responsibility has never faltered.

At 11:00 a.m., another update flashes on my phone. This time, it's Hussam.

"This is it. We're gathering for the departure. It's a total mess. People are exhausted."

After a final round of discussions, the anti-Assad fighters obtained a last-minute authorization to leave with light weapons, mainly Kalashnikovs. Hussam is relieved.

"These weapons are protection, if only psychologically. Who knows what's waiting for us—are they going to try to arrest us? To execute us?" he anxiously confides via

WhatsApp, after furtively connecting to the government-run internet network, accessible from the bus departure point.

A few minutes later, he sends me photos taken on the spot. The last holdouts, faces pale and lips dry, are huddled at the foot of a destroyed building. A film of dust coats their clothes. They've placed their meager belongings at their feet. Each resident has been allowed one bag only. Some have resorted to old flour sacks.

Hussam has just a backpack. He prepared in a rush, filling it with the essentials: a few pairs of pants, a couple of T-shirts, a laptop.

"And of course, the two books Zeina gave me," he adds.

He left everything else behind: cigarette butts in an ashtray, unwashed dishes, a mattress on the floor in the apartment where he and some friends had been hiding out recently, next to the media center. In his haste, he had one final survival instinct.

"I ripped up my notebooks and burned all the documents that had to do with the revolution. Pamphlets, slogans, everything. I can't carry everything with me, and no way was I gonna leave traces of our work for agents of the regime."

Before heading to the bus, he stopped at the cemetery. He met Ahmad, Shadi, and all the others there, on this ribbon of land that has grown longer and longer over the four years of the blockade. Together, they hummed a goodbye song to the city's some two thousand martyrs: friends, brothers-in-arms, fighters, neighbors, all struck down by bombs and war.

It's nearly 5:00 p.m. After over three hours of waiting, the buses are finally preparing to leave.

"Leaving soon!" announces a text message.

I receive a photo taken from inside one of the buses. A blurry selfie with bad lighting, but it's clear enough for me to recognize their thinned faces amid rows of blue seats. Their features and shirts alike are wrinkled by exhaustion and heat. In the middle of the group, the unshakable Hussam flashes his usual mischievous smile. And still, his face has never looked so drawn.

Taken just before the bus departs, this is the last image I'll receive from Daraya.

For hours, silence takes the place of text messages. A wait, as familiar as it is persistent, stretches out like an elastic band. One hundred eighty-six miles is long. Imagine 186 miles punctuated by control stations, over roads pitted by bombs, along routes shaped by the vagaries of war. One hundred eighty-six miles under close escort, under the menacing blades of regime helicopters.

And then, upon waking, a sign of life, the call I was afraid to hope for.

"We've arrived in Idlib!"

It's Hussam who announces the news. Cast out of his home, his city, but relieved to be alive. Despite his exhaustion, at seven in the morning the young man is already making jokes.

"When they woke me up, I immediately asked for grilled chicken! That's how much I've dreamed about it. But my friends told me it was breakfast time. They said I'd waited four years to eat chicken, so I could wait four more hours!"

His laughter is contagious. Behind him, a joyful commotion rings out. I hear the honking of car horns, the jingling of a vegetable seller's cart, the voices of passersby haggling over a few potatoes. Life, real life. And also the first time that we talk without being interrupted by the roar of weapons.

After the sounds come the images. During the evacuation, Shadi couldn't resist the temptation to film, using the camera from the media center, which he slipped into his bag right before leaving.

In the video he sends, through a slightly cracked bus window, I see regime soldiers in khaki fatigues. Their threatening gazes from faces of marble. The bus starts, brushing past scraggly palm trees, driving down long, fractured roads. Mounds of rocks everywhere. Houses flattened like pancakes. A small sample, reaching me by proxy, of the ravages of the conflict.

Then the landscape changes abruptly as they go through a checkpoint. I make out a sign that makes me shiver: Mezzeh, the famous military zone from which the Fourth Division soldiers tirelessly penned in the rebels of Daraya.

Now that they are in regime territory, the road is perfectly paved. Intact apartment buildings stretch out as far as the eye can see. Some curious onlookers on balconies silently watch the procession of buses. The convoy stops, then starts again. Outside, the cars are sparkling. I recognize a few international brands of kitchen appliances on store banners. A portrait of the forbidding Bashar al-Assad is visible in the distance.

The stream of images breaks off again before resuming, this time with rows of spectators applauding the buses' arrival, as if they are champions of the Tour de France. The contrast is dramatic. The streets are euphoric, filled with people greeting the newcomers with the "V for Victory" sign. The men clap as the women begin to make ululations. Teenagers hold up welcome signs. Bright faces and gleaming smiles in every direction.

The book collectors of Daraya have reached safe ground, one of Syria's last rebel strongholds, and their final destination.

"This is Idlib," says Shadi.

On September 12, two weeks after the forced evacuation of Daraya, a video sweeps away any lingering hope for Daraya's campaign of resistance. A confident Bashar al-Assad parades through the deserted streets of the ghost city, followed by the attentive gaze of government cameras. The day after his fifty-first birthday, which coincides with the Muslim celebration of Eid al-Adha, the Syrian leader has given himself quite a gift. Surrounded by a legion of political advisers, military officers, and religious dignitaries, he first leads a collective prayer, then dramatic music rises around him as he poses before the skeletons of the dead city. A smile on his lips, he wears a light gray suit, his neck extending from the collar of an open shirt. He reiterates his standard message: "We are determined to take back every inch of Syria from the terrorists' hands." With the same warlike cadence, he addresses the "sellouts" and "traitors," victims of a "foreign plot." "We are here," he hammers, "to take back that false impression of freedom they wanted to establish at the beginning of the revolution, and to restore true freedom." In four years, his discourse hasn't changed one iota. A narrative woven of the same manufactured threads: "security," "rebuilding," "national prestige," etc.

Here lies Daraya. Crushed by the boots of propaganda. Over the city's lifeless body, and those of its hundreds of martyrs, one narrative replaces another. Vengeful. Bellicose. Lacking in nuance. Bashar al-Assad triumphant, describing the bombardment of Daraya as an antiterrorist offensive, for self-defense. Its forced evacuation wasn't a means to seize new territory, but a vital necessity, he insists. It's time for Syria to regain its former global standing, to become a nation again. For the state to reassert its authority. For the people to fall in line. A question of life or death. For the sake of the country's independence. Of an image to be restored. Assad's famous two options: "Me or chaos."

As a new vocabulary washes over Daraya, the first bits of information about the library start to filter out. The books didn't end up in a bonfire, as Ahmad feared. But it might be worse: after unearthing the secret library, regime soldiers pillaged it to sell the books for cheap on the sidewalk of a flea market in Damascus. Culture at a discount. Four years of saving Daraya's heritage swapped for a few coins.

"I heard the news from friends in Damascus. They

immediately recognized the books with their owners' names, which we'd written on every first page," Ahmad tells me from his new home in Idlib.

He sends me a photo of the destroyed basement. The shot was taken by one of the rare reporters granted access to Daraya, under the regime's close surveillance. I recognize the enclosed space with its perfectly lined-up aisles and wooden shelves along the walls. They're half-empty. The remaining books were thrown on the floor, abandoned to dust and darkness. Ripped-out drawers litter the ground, mixed with scattered volumes. In the background, a soldier wearing fatigues tramples the paper wreckage. His back is to the camera, undoubtedly so he can't be recognized. His intrusive silhouette takes me back to the first image of Daraya I ever saw, the photo from Humans of Syria. What a contrast to the library's previous calm, to the hope spread by the book collectors. The dream of a better world that never fully came true.

I question Ahmad, "So it's over?"

His reply is instantaneous. "Of course not! You can destroy a city. Not ideas!"

He continues: "In Daraya, the regime did its best to erase every positive and intellectual trace of the revolution. To Assad, a cultivated and educated man is a dangerous man, because he represents a challenge to the established order.

But I've grown from this tragedy. I've never felt so free, carrying memories that nobody can take away from me."

Ahmad takes a deep breath, swimming in his thoughts. He's not finished. Not yet. This young man who had so little interest in reading just five years ago cites a historical example dating back to the Mongolian invasion of Iraq, something he learned about while reading during the blockade: the destruction of the Grand Library of Baghdad. In that distant era, the conquerors threw scores of books about medicine and astronomy into the Tigris.

"But they say that the water soaked up so much ink that it changed color," he continues.

The books bled into the river, a metaphor for the abiding resistance of words, even when destroyed.

His account takes me back to another, more contemporary moment in history, which I share in turn. The Bebelplatz of Berlin. It was May 10, 1933. In one night, Hitler's government burned thousands of dissenting works seized by Nazi troops. Among the paper victims were the so-called subversive writings of Stefan Zweig, Karl Marx, Bertolt Brecht, and also Sigmund Freud. That night, Joseph Goebbels, the minister of propaganda, gave a speech on the creation of a new world. A world in which books hostile to the regime would no longer have the right to exist.

Years later, in 1995, the Israeli sculptor Micha Ullman, whose parents had fled Berlin, returned to that square. He created a ghost library under the pavestones in memory of the book burning. Covered by a glass ceiling, buried in the ground, the space is deliberately empty. Impossible to access. You have to stand above it, lean over, to contemplate this space—fifty square meters filled with white, empty shelves. The installation is known as *Versunkene Bibliothek*: the Sunken Library.

Will Daraya, like Berlin, have its own Bebelplatz one day? What will remain of its underground library tomorrow, the day after tomorrow, in half a century? Once its many devastated houses have been razed to the ground, will the rebel suburb, once famous for its delicious white grapes, be transformed into a military base, as rumors say? Bashar al-Assad's goal was to disfigure the city. Burn its fields. Make its landscape unrecognizable. Erase all of Daraya's pages, empty sentences of their remaining words.

I tell myself that, whatever may come, these young Syrian heroes have an indestructible story to share. Facing the destruction of bombs, they didn't just save books. They created a new vocabulary—*shelli, karkabeh*—and played with the rules of grammar. Day and night, they never stopped believing in the power and invincibility of speech. They broke the silence and took up the story.

With their books and slogans and magazines, their graf-fiti and literary creations, they resisted the rigid verses of war, beating out a cadence that wasn't cannon fire. Words versus violence. A language of peace and survival for the next generation.

EPILOGUE

Istanbul, August 26, 2017

I often have the same dream, which is both sweet and odd. It's story time. Samarra and I are skipping across Istanbul's cobbled alleys. Taksim Square and its *simit* seller watch us go by. Above our heads, seagulls fly off in the direction of summer. At the Istiklal Avenue entrance, the main door of the French Institute is now blocked. To access the building, we have to go through a security gate, located on an adjacent street. But we still enter the library from the back of the main garden. Along the ramp of the staircase that descends into the arena of books, someone has put up mandalas, along with the word "hope."

Julie the storyteller is waiting for us at the bottom of the steps, index finger against her lips. "Surprise!" she exclaims. We enter. Across from the children's bench, three adults have taken their places. I immediately recognize the figures as Ahmad, Shadi, and Hussam. "We've come to tell you the extraordinary story of a secret library," they whisper to their young audience, which is immediately won over. At the end of their account, the little spectators receive a gift—books with empty pages. All are invited to write or draw the story of Daraya.

In my dream, the contours of these young men's faces are incredibly precise. Never, during our countless virtual conversations over these past few years, had I been able to make out the texture of their skin, the delicateness of their features, the color of their eyes. But in the dream, every detail is here. Voices. Gestures. Expressions.

My dream is no longer a fantasy, inspired by brief exchanges between one explosion and the next. My dream is now a continuation of reality, of reunions on Turkish soil that we hadn't dared to hope would happen, of face-to-face encounters that have strengthened our unique friendships.

One year has gone by since their hurried departure from Daraya. One year of trying to distance themselves from the nightmarish absurdity of what they lived through. A year of staring life right in the eye, looking at the world through something other than a smartphone screen. Of traveling, too. One after the other, they slowly broke the shell, some venturing beyond the Syrian border.

Shadi was the first to set foot outside Syria. In October 2016, he arrived in Reyhanli, in the province of Hatay, in southwest Turkey. The Turkish government, which has welcomed over 2.5 million Syrian exiles into its territory, granted him a travel permit to have an operation on his hand. He offered to meet me in a coffee shop in the small Turkish town, where many Syrians had found refuge. When I arrived, I immediately identified Shadi by the bandage covering his left arm. He had a leather jacket and short, slightly slicked-back hair. The encounter was strange—this was our first time meeting in person, and yet it felt like we had just spoken the night before. The waiter, a Syrian from Aleppo, led us to a small table, setting down two glasses of tea. With his right hand, the uninjured one, Shadi opened a bag he'd been carrying over his shoulder. One of the few belongings he'd brought from Daraya. He took out an object and set it on the table: his camera. The one that had saved his life. I didn't say anything. I looked at the charred lens as you would a survivor. In one slow movement, he swept off the dust still covering the device.

"How are you?"

It was as if he hadn't heard my question.

"Daraya was a symbol," said Shadi. "This camera was the witness. Sadly, the entire world has abandoned us . . ."

Sitting at this café table, face still worn by exhaustion, he was carrying the pain of his city. I asked him if he'd seen the video of Bashar al-Assad in Daraya.

"All a show!" he replied.

He bent over his bag again. It was full of hard drives: all the photos and videos saved during four years of siege.

"These are the images of Daraya that I don't want to forget," he insisted. "Images of a united, bonded group. Of a common desire to build the future. To defend new ideas in development. We were one and the same. The same feeling of solidarity, of camaraderie. A unique experience that could have served as a model for other towns. Daraya isn't just a place, it's a philosophy of life."

Shadi was lost in his memories, gaze tinged with nostalgia. He talked about Daraya as if it had been an adventure. If he had to do it over, he continued, he wouldn't hesitate a second.

"Today, Bashar al-Assad is trying to make us the losers. For me, the fact that we were able to hang on for four years during such a cruel siege is already a huge victory."

Behind us, a customer opened the door to the little café, which also served as a pastry shop. Arms full of presents, she hesitated, debating out loud between a cake inspired by *Frozen* and one by *Cinderella* for her daughter's birthday. Shadi smiled.

"The hardest," he said, "is afterward. Now we have to learn to live normally, to watch planes go by without trembling, to fall asleep in silence." Shadi, used to the fleetingness of life in Daraya, where everything had been dictated by falling bombs, seemed unmoored.

"Suddenly, everything's permanent again, like it's going to last forever. Our notions of time, space, everything, have changed. Life is organized, there's no fear, no dangers. Everything's so disconcertingly simple."

A few weeks later, I called Shadi to see how he was doing. The surgery had gone well. He had begun to regain some motor function in his fingers and the doctor had prescribed physical therapy sessions. During his convalescence, he had temporarily moved to Istanbul, where his parents migrated a few years ago. His mother stuffs him with fish and his father is dissuading him from going back to Syria. Shadi remains persuaded that his place is still there. For now, he's taking Turkish lessons and plans to resume his studies. Once a month, we meet up over coffee, and we *shelli* in memory of Daraya.

After countless failed attempts at virtual conversations during the Daraya blockade, Ustez and I finally saw each other face-to-face in Istanbul in January 2017. He had come to Turkey to recharge his batteries for a bit. Sitting in a restaurant in Taksim Square, Muhammad Shihadeh was exactly how I had imagined him: calm, poised, generous with his time and his words. For three hours, he talked about how civic engagement began in Daraya. About this unique experience that stretched back to the nineties, and for which he had been one of the driving forces. About his favorite books. About the poems of Mahmoud Darwish and the self-help works he was so fond of. As I listened to him, his powerful influence on the young people of Daraya became even clearer to me. When I told him just how grateful they had been to him, he blushed. "Oh, they're the ones who taught me. I'm a very serious person. They were far funnier than I was. When I was with them, I would forget my worries."

But now the traumas of the siege are eclipsed by other concerns, paradoxically harder to overcome: How to view the future? How to understand the divisions ripping Syria apart? How to avoid sinking into pessimism when the fate of the 2011 revolutionaries is becoming even more elusive?

"Despite the difficulty of the siege, we were living with the stubborn hope of something better. Suddenly, a new reality is setting in, full of uncertainty."

And then Ustez said something that I've never forgotten:

"The siege paradoxically protected us from any attempt at radicalization. It allowed us to keep the spirit of Daraya alive. For four years, it was just us. It wasn't easy all the time, but we always settled our differences through dialogue. There was no external invasion. No attempts at manipulation. No foreign intrusion. A singular experience."

This is far from the case in other regions of Syria, where foreign and regional powers are defending their factions,

interests, and parcels of land. At the whim of shifting al-
liances, groups are formed, disbanded, transformed, rad-
icalized. One year after the fall of Daraya, the country is
on the verge of partition. As Daesh clings to the remaining
areas under its control, and the Kurdish minority tries to
protect its enclave, Bashar al-Assad is doing his best to re-
conquer the last moderate rebel bastions one by one with
the support of his Russian and Syrian allies. After Daraya
came East Aleppo, Al-Waer, and then Barzeh. The region
of Idlib, to where thousands of civilians and fighters from
the Free Syrian Army, forced to surrender, were evacuated,
has once again become the end of the line of the anti-Assad
revolt.

Despite the uncertainty weighing on his country's future, Ustez went back to northern Syria in the spring of
2017. In May, good news brightened his return. His wife
and children, refugees in Damascus since the closing of
the last access point into Daraya, in early 2016, were able
to join him in Idlib. And for the first time, he kissed the
youngest of his three children, born during the siege.

Hussam is doing well, true to his optimistic nature. In late
2016, he crossed the border with the help of a smuggler and
settled in Gaziantep, in southern Turkey. Shortly after ar-
riving, he gave up his pseudonym in favor of his original

name, Jihad. This is a common name in the Levant, without any specific religious affiliation. In January 2017, he contacted me from Istanbul. He'd arrived in the city the day before to visit Zeina and meet his future in-laws. Jihad was staying in a little hotel on Istiklal, the legendary pedestrian avenue where the French Institute is located. I met him in a café, a few feet from the sidewalk targeted last year by a suicide bomber. I didn't say anything. I didn't want to spoil his enthusiasm. Jihad was in awe of everything. The perfectly aligned monuments. The quality of public transportation. The electricity working without a hitch. In only one day, he had already found all the best places in town. He had eaten a pizza at Eataly and made a round of the second-hand bookshops, where he splurged on a dozen books, including *Pride and Prejudice*, Jane Austen's famous novel about the institution of marriage in England in the early nineteenth century. His passion for reading, born during the blockade, drew him to the historic, recently renovated, Beyazit State Library. He even found the time to dart into Pages, an old wooden house turned into a bookstore frequented by young Syrian artists and intellectuals, in the heart of the Fatih neighborhood, the "Little Damascus" of Istanbul.

After two strong espressos in the café on Istiklal, Jihad stood up. He had to take care of a few "administrative issues." I went with him. During these meetings full of sleight of hand and bills slipped into jacket pockets, I recognized the resourceful and risk-taking "Hussam" from Daraya. A few hours later, his visa had already been extended, with a guarantee he would receive his residency card. Then we took a taxi to the official Syrian consulate, perched in a chic neighborhood, where he had to renew his passport. Jihad was anxious, haunted by an intense fear of being watched by the regime. A cousin living in Damascus had given him the name of a civil servant that he could whisper in the ear of a government employee. Jihad had barely crossed the entryway when he was welcomed with a warm hug and the promise of new papers in less than a month. The benefits of *wasta*, string-pulling Middle Eastern–style, even between the worst of enemies.

"After the nightmare we lived through, nothing surprises me anymore and nothing scares me anymore," Jihad said, laughing, as we left the meeting.

That same evening, he was already on an overnight bus to Gaziantep, where he was scheduled to take an exam the next day in the hopes of joining an NGO. His resilience was rewarded. Despite the exhaustion of traveling, and the masses of technical information to absorb in a short amount of time, the test went well. His new life could begin. But without Zeina. A few weeks later, Jihad discreetly broke off his engagement with his fiancée. He wanted, no doubt, to rebuild himself before starting a family. Even with the best intentions in the world, a four-year siege can't be processed in a few months.

Omar, aka Ibn Khaldun, lives in memory. In thought. In conversation. In the videos and photos kept by his comrades. Following the evacuation of the city, in late August 2016, the negotiation committee was able to recover his body as part of an exchange of remains between the Free Syrian Army and the Fourth Division. Omar was finally buried alongside his own people, in the cemetery of martyrs in Daraya. A hole in the dust, a name engraved on a headstone, and a few flowers as a final tribute. There, on the land for which he fought, in this small bastion of insurrection at the gates of Damascus, the Syrian sleeper in the valley rests for eternity, like Rimbaud's soldier. He sleeps in the sun, his hand on his chest. Peaceful. Feet in the gladiolas. Body in a shroud of ruins.

Like Abu el-Ezz and Abu Malek al-Shami, Ahmad chose to stay in Idlib, his new home, for lack of options. He shares a small house with his siege comrades in a small town on the Turkish border. He reads a lot, volunteers to help displaced populations, and finds solace in walking through olive groves and listening to the *Amélie* soundtrack on repeat. And yet this is far from a refuge. In late 2016, like an endlessly repeating nightmare, Ahmad vicariously lived through the end of another siege, this time of the rebel suburb of East Aleppo, as he watched Idlib be flooded by a new wave of displaced people, faces dazed and dreams broken from a similar deluge of bombs. In April 2017, the chemical attack on Khan Sheikhoun, in the province of Idlib, also reopened the wounds of Daraya.

"I was paralyzed when I heard the news. It's like someone pressed the replay button. I was reliving what we endured in 2013," confides Ahmad.

A few days later, the new U.S. president, Donald Trump, retaliated with strikes on positions held by the Syrian regime. Then the resumption of the Astana talks brought an end to Russian-Syrian aerial bombings. In accordance with a still-vague deal signed in May 2017, Moscow, Tehran, and Ankara have gambled on making Idlib one of four new so-called de-escalation zones to establish a lasting truce there between pro- and anti-Assad factions.

But anxiety over an uncertain future settled over the relief brought by this semblance of a truce. Initially welcomed as heroes, Daraya's activists are growing disenchanted. "We wanted to embody a third path, to show that an alternative to the regime and Daesh was possible."

But in northwestern Syria, the mood is different and the situation more complex: "In Daraya, activists and combatants interacted. Here, military factions want to control all civil initiatives."

While there may still be an active moderate armed opposition, the most radical groups, such as the jihadists of the former al-Nusra Front, are imposing their law. They tear down the opposition's flags. Tag walls with religious slogans. Repress demonstrations. Forbid women's voices from radio broadcasts.

These pressures are only distancing Ahmad from religion even more. He shaved his beard, opposes the idea of a compulsory veil for Syrian woman, and condemns the hypocrisy of extremists.

"Those people don't represent Islam. The other day, a guy close to al-Nusra asked me to help him fix his cell phone. The Islamic profession of faith was plastered across the screen. But his files were full of pornographic movies . . ."

In reality, Idlib province is a big *karkabeh*, he admits. There's no longer a precise goal, a defined objective. Dozens of factions and local councils are engaged in stiff competition. There's also the omnipresent fear that the regime will make this the site of its final sweep. That the sole remaining bastion of the rebellion will be the theater for the last battle against the insurgents.

Yet Ahmad wants to remain hopeful. Convinced that the long night of the Syrian people will be followed by a rebirth. In what form? He doesn't know. In the meantime, he has launched a mobile library for the children of Idlib. On nights of doubt and uncertainty, he thinks back to the unique experience of Daraya.

A few days ago, Ahmad dug up a video on his smartphone. On August 27, 2016, two hours before leaving the besieged enclave, he crossed the ruins of his city alone, filming his steps along with all the destroyed houses and buildings that now resembled construction sites laid to waste. The video ends with a shot of the shell-battered facade of the library.

"When I think about Daraya, this is the picture etched in my mind. In my head, I watch it stream by in black and white to the rhythm of Mahmoud Darwish's voice reading *State of Siege*."

It's an unforgettable image. Ahmad's final memory of Daraya's incredible, unexpected library sanctuary.

THE BOOK COLLECTORS
OF DARAYA

© Asli Akinci

Ahmad Muaddamani is a cofounder of Daraya's secret library. Born in 1993, Ahmad was a student of civil engineering before the war. From the start of the Syrian uprising, he participated in revolutionary activities, and when the siege began, he joined the media center run by the local council. After the forced evacuation of Daraya, he launched and managed a mobile library in the province of Idlib with a group of friends. He now lives in Gaziantep, Turkey, where he works for a number of peacebuilding and humanitarian programs focusing on Syria.

Omar Abu Anas was born in 1992 in Daraya. His engineering studies were interrupted by the 2011 revolution, in which he actively participated. When violence erupted, Omar joined the Free Syrian Army, taking up arms to protect the inhabitants of Daraya against the brutality of the regime. A peacemaker at heart, he always believed in the power of books and was one of the first of the book collectors to gather and bring them to the basement that later became a secret library. In 2016, one month before the end of the siege, Omar was killed by a regime strike.

Born in 1991, Shadi Matar participated in the 2011 street demonstrations despite his parents' fear and opposition. When the siege started, he joined the media center of Daraya and started taking photos and videos as a citizen journalist eager to document the war. In the absence of independent and foreign media, his work provided a picture different from the regime propaganda. In July 2016, he was injured by a mortar shell. Immediately after the end of the siege, Shadi came to Turkey to undergo surgery. After three years in Istanbul, where his parents live, he was granted asylum in France. He now lives in Bordeaux, where he is hoping to resume his studies to become a professional cameraman.

© Delphine Minoui

Hussam Ayash (Jihad Dalein) was born in Daraya in 1984. He became an active member of the Daraya local council and its media center soon after the revolution. Passionate about books, especially psychology and self-help, he also participated in launching a local magazine called *Karkabeh* during the siege. After being evacuated to Idlib, where he lived for a few months, he moved to Gaziantep, Turkey, where he married a young Syrian activist from Raqqa. He works for an NGO helping the Syrian White Helmets of the Civil Defense.

Abu Malek al-Shami, nicknamed "the Banksy of Syria," brought light to the city by painting graffiti and murals on its ruins. A cofounder of Daraya's library, Abu Malek al-Shami is among those who still live in Idlib, the last rebel stronghold, which the Syrian regime, backed by Russia and Iran, is trying to regain. His paints remain his best weapon: he designs new murals for Idlib's buildings that have been destroyed by the barrel bombs.

Abu el-Ezz (Ezzat Kassas), born in 1993, is one of the cofounders of Daraya's secret library, in which he actively participated, first as a book-rescuer, then as a codirector. In 2015, he was severely injured by a barrel bomb attack while on his way to the underground library. Shortly after recovering, he insisted on resuming his work, eager to promote education and culture in the face of war. Today, Abu el-Ezz lives in Istanbul.

© Marie Tihon

U stez (Muhammad Shihadeh), forty-two, is one of the
pillars of the Daraya Shebab (Daraya Youth), a group
of activists who, in the 1990s, launched a series of peaceful initiatives to inspire democratic values in Syrian society. Their vision of nonviolent resistance had a crucial
impact on Daraya's new generation of activists during the
siege. Nicknamed "Ustez," or "Professor," Muhammad
Shihadeh supported the young revolutionaries through
his wisdom, advice, and English classes. He now lives with
his family in Gaziantep, where he works as a freelance
translator.

Daraya's underground library was a collective dream, realized through the involvement of many, including the essential contributions of Homam al-Toun, Ayman al-Toun, Saed Sakka, Maher Khoulani, Muhammad al-Dabbas, Amer Kattan, Rami Sakka, Muhammad Abu Ubada, Abdul Basit al-Ahmar, Malik Alrifaii, Ayham Sakka, Rateb Abu el-Fouz, and countless other anonymous heroes who kept the light of Daraya shining by saving books and celebrating education.

READERS' FAVORITES FROM THE LIBRARY AT DARAYA

The Alchemist by Paulo Coelho

Kitab al Ibar (The Book of Lessons) by Ibn Khaldun

The Little Prince by Antoine de Saint-Exupéry

The Shell by Mustafa Khalifa

The Prince by Niccolò Machiavelli

Les Misérables by Victor Hugo

The 7 Habits of Highly Effective People by Stephen Covey

Psychology and You by Julia C. Berryman, Elizabeth M. Ockleford, Kevin Howells, David J. Hargreaves, and Diane J. Wildbur.

Men Are from Mars, Women Are from Venus by John Gray

State of Siege by Mahmoud Darwish

ALSO MENTIONED:

"A Sleeper in the Valley" by Arthur Rimbaud
poetry of Nizar Qabbani
Syrian theologian Ibn Qayyim
theater of Shakespeare and Molière
Marcel Proust
J. M. Coetzee
Fahrenheit 451 by Ray Bradbury
1984 by George Orwell

ACKNOWLEDGMENTS

I could only keep half my promise: this book is finally out in the world, but it won't find a place, as I had hoped, on the shelves of the library in Daraya, back under regime control.

These pages now belong to Ahmad, Shadi, Jihad (alias Hussam), Abu Malek al-Shami, Abu el-Ezz, and their faithful siege companions. They are a testament to their commitment to peaceful resistance and their unflagging desire for life and democracy, which they defended to the end.

I want to express my infinite gratitude for their trust and their availability. In the lulls of their war, they never stopped wanting to bear witness.

I'd also like to thank Muhammad Shihadeh, the irreplaceable Ustez, for his generosity and openness during our long discussions when he came to Istanbul. Our conversations allowed me to clarify certain facts and more clearly understand Daraya's unique situation and history.

As I was writing this book, I relied on the professionalism and enthusiasm of two outstanding young Syrian interpreters and, at the time, aspiring reporters, Sarah Dadouch and Asmaa al Omar. Invariably patient and receptive, they demonstrated an exceptional work ethic and great attentiveness, including when translating messages sent, however early in the morning or late at night, from Daraya. I have no doubt that Sarah and Asmaa will make phenomenal reporters, thanks to their love of country and passion for journalism.

The Book Collectors wouldn't have ended up in its current form without the encouragement of the Spanish novelist Luisa Etxenike. She was a precious source of aid when I was haunted by the eternal question of how to make the invisible visible, and grappling with how best to shape this story.

The faithful first reader of many of my books, my friend the filmmaker Katia Jarjoura, provided, once again, a critical and objective perspective on my work. I am incredibly grateful for her help.

I'm particularly indebted to Hala Moughania for her thoughtful and detailed feedback. Her insightful comments proved invaluable.

I'd also like to warmly thank my researcher friend Carole André-Dessornes for her advice and kind support.

Finally, I want to end this book with a special thought for Omar, the young rebel-reader gone too soon, and for his dreams cut short. I hope his memory allows his family and friends to find the strength necessary to continue their quest for freedom.

A NOTE ABOUT THE TRANSLATOR

Lara Vergnaud is a translator of prose, creative nonfiction, and scholarly works from the French. She is the recipient of two PEN/Heim Translation Fund Grants and a French Voices Grand Prize, and has been nominated for the National Translation Award. She lives in Washington, DC.

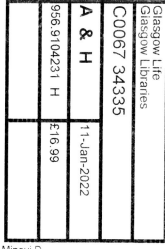

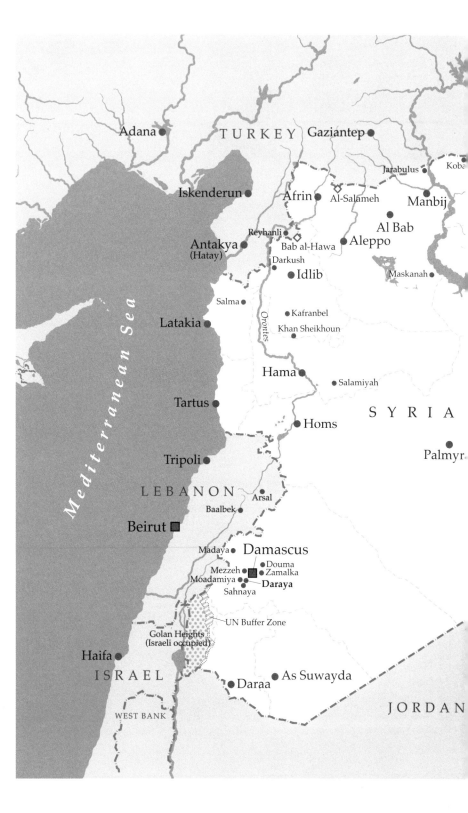